HISTORY UNSCHOOLED INVENTIONS FROM THE BRONZE AGE

BY JJ CARROLL

HISTORY UNSCHOOLED
INVENTIONS FROM THE BRONZE AGE

First Published in the United States by Quality Business Communications, Inc., Reading, Pennsylvania, USA. 2023

ISBN: 978-1-7328147-6-9

ACKNOWLEDGEMENTS

For Diane, my sister, former homeschooler and fellow lover of history, whose never-ending support and ideas keep me going every day!

TABLE OF CONTENTS

HOW TO USE THIS BOOK

Students will learn history through human inventions

It has long been true that necessity is the mother of invention. Since the dawn of our species, we've been thinking and creating based on our needs and lifestyles. This book will help students learn about the Bronze Age by studying the most important discoveries of the times.

The UN-textbook helps students think on their own

The concept is to allow students to think and learn without a textbook full of facts to memorize (and quickly forget after the quiz). Instead, kids can immerse themselves in stories to get in the mindset.

Then, they'll find thought provoking questions and topics to research, write about and discuss. How they do that is up to you... or them. Should they write an essay? Take sides in a formal debate? Or simply discuss over dinner?

Encourage reading, writing and research along the way

This book encourages all types of reading and writing as well as oral presentations. Besides the lists of fiction and nonfiction books, each chapter has opportunities for writing, critical thinking, research and discussion.

Research is an important life skill for anyone to have regardless of whether a student is college bound. Learn more about research skills on page 4. You may wish to start there before you begin the historic units, especially with older students. They'll have ample opportunity to use their newfound research skills throughout the year.

Have fun with STEAM-based activities

Since each topic is an invention, it was easy to incorporate Science, Technology, Engineering, Art, and Math into the learning.

Look for these icons in the Activities section of each chapter.

Science

Technology

Engineering

Art

Mathematics

The whole family can learn together

If you have multiple students in various grades, they all can learn together. Each invention chapter includes family-friendly activities at all education levels:

> **Level 1** indicates easy activities for elementary students.
> **Level 2** involves more reading and simple research skills for middle school ages.
> **Level 3** encourages a higher level of research and writing skills for high school age students.

You or your older students can choose to do all of the activities, or just those on the higher levels.

How historic novels help kids learn about different times

Fiction is a great way to get kids interested in a topic. Especially when the alternative is a textbook. These fictional stories are for kids to experience the past. The education part should be subtle. The side effect? Kids who read!

We include a list of recommended fiction (and movies) that take place during, or focus on a certain aspect of, the Bronze Age. Feel free to add to the list if you know of books that we missed or as new books are published. Ask your librarian or local bookstore owner for suggestions.

You can allow students to absorb the history on their own. Or you can have your own family book club and discuss the stories as well. Talk about the inventions learned, or challenge them to research and discuss any suspected fallacies in the stories. Fiction means it's not all fact. Students can have fun busting myths and catching where the author took creative license.

Print out answer sheets, coloring pages and more

Be sure to download and print our FREE History Unschooled Bronze Age Print Pack to get hotlinks to the resources, plus printable worksheets and all the activity pages in this book to help you sort and store written materials for your homeschool record keeping.

Scan this QR code to get the History Unschooled: Inventions from the Bronze Age print pack:

TIPS TO ACCESS THE NOVELS AND OTHER BOOKS FOR FREE

Look for the suggested movies and books at your local library. If not available, your librarian may be able to request it in from a sister library.

If your child has a smart device and can download apps, consider a membership with Libby, which works through the library system to lend eBooks for free.

You might also check used book stores in your area or online, such as Thriftbooks.com, to get books at a discounted price.

Historic Books for Kids is a proud supporter of *your* local bookstore.

If FREE or discount isn't available, you can buy online AND support local at the same time. Historic Books for Kids bookshop uses **Bookshop.org** (https://bookshop.org/info/about-us), which is a nonprofit organization that supports local brick and mortar book stores instead of mega online retailers.

Most of the books listed on pages 9 and 10 are available at:

https://bookshop.org/shop/HistoricBooksforKids.

HOW TO RESEARCH HISTORIC TOPICS

Research is a process not an action

The goal of research is to fully understand the source data and satisfactorily answer questions as accurately as possible.

Typically the process goes like this:

1. **Ask your question**
2. **Choose your sources and gather data**
3. **Sort and process the information**
4. **Develop your answer**
5. **Cite your sources**

Ask your question

What is it you want to know? This is where you plan your investigation. Be prepared to change or form new questions as you uncover facts.

For example, you want to know who invented the wheel. As you perform your research, you realize that the wheel existed before recorded history. That means you probably won't ever be able to answer "who" specifically invented it. The answer doesn't exist.

But you might be able to determine approximately when it was invented based on archaeological evidence. You may also learn the oldest evidence of use to conclude where it was likely invented. This can help narrow down your search to a specific species, people or tribe.

Choose your sources and gather data

There are three kinds of sources:

1. **Primary**
2. **Secondary**
3. **Tertiary**

1. Primary Source:

Direct evidence about your topic. This includes things like archaeological evidence, account books (such as the *Domesday Book*), boat passenger lists, diaries and other contemporary writings. "Contemporary" means it was written or recorded by someone who personally witnessed the event, experienced the time, or created the data.

The reference section of a library may lead you to Primary sources. You can also consult:

> Library of Congress at
> https://www.loc.gov/programs/teachers/getting-started-with-primary-sources/finding/

> National Archives at
> https://www.archives.gov/education/research/primary-sources

> Smithsonian at
> https://learninglab.si.edu/collections/primary-sources/MhkNadPOAl59VFw1

2. *Secondary Source:*

A commentary or interpretation of a primary source, such as a journal article or news story. This type of source includes retellings from someone who was not present during the event, even if the person was alive at the time.

3. *Tertiary Source:*

This third level source can refer to someone else's assembly of information based on consolidated primary and secondary sources. Wikipedia, academic papers, magazine articles, and blog posts fall into this category.

Tertiary sources can help guide students to primary and secondary sources through their citations. Parents and teachers might encourage Level 2 students to use and cite trusted tertiary sources while encouraging Level 3 students to consult the primary sources for themselves to make their own interpretation.

Sort and process the information

Four blind men found an animal. One touched a leg and was sure he found a goat. One found the tail and thought it was a giraffe. One felt the fur and believed it was a dog. The last had the belly and thought it was a horse. None of them had the whole picture; therefore they couldn't agree on the type of animal they had found. The hungry lion ate them all.

No single source should lead you to a final conclusion because no single source will have all the data. There's an old saying that history was written by the victors. That means the stories you hear about antiquity – even when told by a primary source – can be incomplete, one-sided or wrong, especially if the author had an agenda or prejudice.

An agenda refers to why something was written. What purpose did it serve? Who did the writing and for whom did they write?

A prejudice can refer to the author's leanings and if they wanted someone in the story to look bad – or good.

Agendas and prejudices can impact how the story was told, including omissions, exaggerations, and outright fiction. Secondary sources are based on interpretations and often hearsay, which can likewise be wrong. Sometimes the wrong story can be passed down for generations.

Consider the story of young George Washington chopping down a cherry tree and telling the truth about it to his father. For nearly two centuries, Americans believed it as hardcore fact. It wasn't until a researcher noticed there was no primary source for the story. In fact, the first time it was written was after Washington's death. The public was hungry for information about their hero and a minister and bookseller named Mason Locke Weems delivered. He first published Washington's biography in 1800. Then he updated it several times and the cherry tree story was added in the 5th edition in 1806. Washington did have a reputation for honesty and maybe Weems wanted to encourage honesty for kids. Or maybe he was just looking to sell books with legendary stories. The point is, the cherry tree event probably never happened.

Likewise, there's no actual evidence that famous characters like Robin Hood and King Arthur ever existed. But the stories have some root possibilities for which the primary sources may be lost to antiquity or haven't been found yet.

The key to successful historic research is to consult as many sources as possible. See if primary sources exist and, if so, what different sources have to say. See how their stories differ and how they are the same. Consider any potential prejudices and agendas. Keep in mind what the primary source, data, archaeological dig or other information does NOT tell you.

Then see how different secondary sources interpret the event. Review tertiary sources and decide if you agree with them. If you don't agree, look for evidence to support your disagreement.

Develop your answer

After all that research and myth busting, you can finally draw a conclusion based on the evidence collected. Do you have any questions that remain unanswered due to lack of evidence? Is there enough evidence to support a possibility, even if not certainty? Write your conclusion so it reflects facts only and not your own or someone else's opinion.

Cite your sources

A proper citation gives full credit to the originator of the data and includes enough information to enable a reader to find the source for themselves. Citing your source also gives you the opportunity to reflect on the reliability of the source information.

There are several ways to cite a source. Some methods are for academic use and others are for business. They may also vary by field. Historians usually use citations as presented in *Chicago Manual of Style*. You can find and learn more at https://www.chicagomanualofstyle.org/tools_citationguide.html.

TRY OUT YOUR NEW RESEARCH SKILLS

Legends: Fiction vs. Fact is 32 pages of fun stories that show the importance of research skills. It includes games and a legendary research project kids can try on their own.

Get it on the Historic Books for Kids website (www.historicbooksforkids).

BRONZE AGE

3300 BCE TO 1200 BCE

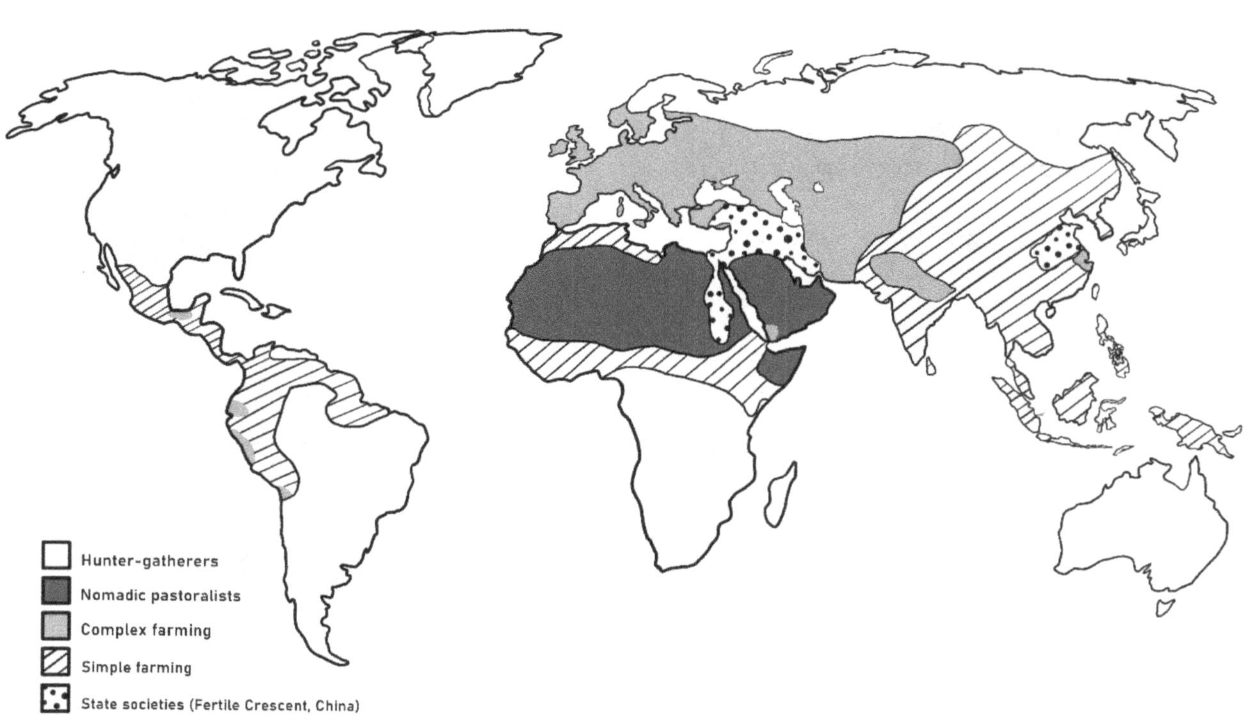

SUGGESTED BOOKS MOVIES AND MORE

Books and movies can help kids learn and become enthusiastic about the Bronze Age. Here is a list of suggested books, movies and more. Kids can also suggest their own. Ask your local librarian for new and popular books that take place during the Bronze Age. Encourage them to talk about the stories and what they learned.

Stories and Novels

- We're Sailing Down the Nile: A Journey Through Egypt by Laurie Krebs (4-7 years)
- The Warlord's Alarm by Virginia Pilegard
- Mummies in the Morning by Mary Pope Osborne (6-9 years)
- Mummy Cat by Marcus Ewert (6-9 years)
- The Egypt Game by Zilpha Keatley Snyder (8 - 11 years)
- The Boy with the Bronze Axe by Kathleen Fidler (8-12 years)
- On the Run in Ancient China by Linda Bailey (8-12 years)
- The Eye of Ra by Ben Gartner (9-12 years)
- The Golden Bull: A Mesopotamia Adventure by Marjorie Cowley (9-12 years)
- Mark of the Thief by Jennifer A. Nielsen (10-12 years)
- Adara by Beatrice Gormley (9-14 years)
- Amber and Clay by Laura Amy Schlitz (10-14 years)
- Black Ships Before Troy: The Story of 'The Iliad' by Rosemary Sutcliff (10-14 years)
- Warrior Scarlett by Rosemary Sutcliff (12-17 years)
- Pharaoh's Daughter: A Novel of Ancient Egypt by Julius Lester

Nonfiction

- Ancient Egypt for Kids: Learn About Pyramids, Mummies, Pharaohs, Gods, and More! by Samuel John. (5-8 years)
- The Story of Clocks and Calendars by Betsy Maestro and Giulio Maestro (6 - 10 years)
- The Secrets of Stonehenge by Mick Manning (7-11 years)
- DK Eyewitness Books: Mesopotamia: Discover the Cradle of Civilization--The Birthplace of Writing, Religion, and the [With Clip-Art CD] by Philip Steele and John Farndon (8-12 years)
- Ancient Science: 40 Time-Traveling, World-Exploring, History-Making Activities for Kids by Jim Wiese (8-12 years)
- Timekeeping: Explore the History and Science of Telling Time with 15 Projects by Linda Formichelli and Maxine Anderson (8 - 12 years)

➢ Shang and Zhou Dynasties: The Bronze Age of China - Early Civilization Ancient History for Kids 5th Grade Social Studies by Baby Professor

➢ Children's Encyclopedia of Ancient History: Step Back in Time to Discover the Wonders of the Stone Age, Ancient Egypt, Ancient Greece, Ancient Rome... by Philip Steele (K-12 grade)

➢ Hands-On History: Ancient Civilizations Activities (Teacher): by Kristi Pikiewicz and Garth Sundem (7-14 years)

➢ Writing History: The Bronze Age by Anita Ganeri (9- 12 years)

➢ Pharaoh's Boat by David Weitzman (10-13 years)

➢ Sea Peoples of the Bronze Age Mediterranean C.1400 BC-1000 BC by Raffaele D'Amato and Andrea Salimbeti (Young adult - adult)

Movies (fiction)

➢ **The Ten Commandments** (1956) Classic American epic about the life of the biblical character Moses and his deliverance of Hebrew slaves from Egypt. Starring Charlton Heston, Yul Brynner, Anne Baxter and Edward G. Robinson; written by Dorothy Clarke Wilson J.H. Ingraham, and A.E. Southon; and directed and narrated by Cecil B. DeMille.

➢ **Jason and the Argonauts** (1963) The legendary Greek hero leads a team of adventurers in the quest for the Golden Fleece. Starring Todd Armstrong, Nancy Kovack, Gary Raymond, and Laurence Naismith; written by Jan Read, Beverley Cross, and Apollonios Rhodiosl; and directed by Don Chaffey.

➢ **The Prince of Egypt** (1998) Animated version of The Ten Commandments story of Moses and Ramses. Starring the voices of Val Kilmer, Ralph Fiennes, and Michelle Pfeiffer; Written by Philip LaZebnik and Nicholas Meyer; directed by Brenda Chapman, Steve Hickner, and Simon Wells.

➢ **The Scorpion King** (2002) In ancient Gomorrah, thousands of years before the Pyramids, the remaining free nomadic tribes are forced to form an uneasy alliance to put an end to mighty King Memnon's reign of tyranny. Starring Dwayne Johnson, Steven Brand and Michael Clarke Duncan; written by Stephen Sommers and Jonathan Hales; and directed by Chuck Russell. Rated PG-13 for intense sequences of action violence and some sensuality.

➢ **Night at the Museum: Secret of the Tomb** (2014) The third installment of the series, when the magic powers of The Tablet of Ahkmenrah begin to die out, Larry Daley unites favorite and new characters while embarking on an epic quest to save the magic before it is gone forever. Starring Ben Stiller, Robin Williams, and Owen Wilson; written by David Guion, Michael Handelman, and Mark Friedman; and directed by Shawn Levy. Rated PG for mild action, some rude humor and brief language.

Documentaries, videos, virtual tours and more (nonfiction).

> Learn about **archaeology** and watch excavations unfold at:
> https://www.archaeological.org/programs/public/interactive-digs/.

> **Ancient Greek Inventions That Are Still Used Today** - WorldAtlas at
> https://www.worldatlas.com/amp/history/ancient-greek-inventions-that-are-still-used-today.html

> Learn about **Structure and Applications of Metals**, including the Egyptian smelting process and more, from Penn State University's online education center, at https://www.e-education.psu.edu/matse81/node/2121 .

> **The Story of Egypt**, an historical documentary told in four episodes, available through Amazon Prime videos.

> Take a virtual tour of the **Papyrus Museum** in Austria at
> https://www.onb.ac.at/en/museums/papyrus-museum/about-the-papyrus-museum/virtual-papyrus-museum.

> Learn about **A Brief History of Books** from Arts and Culture at:
> https://artsandculture.google.com/story/a-brief-history-of-books/OAXR-SPrQmOCew?hl=en.

> Take a virtual tour of **Ancient Mesopotamia** at:
> https://www.youtube.com/watch?v=KfZi4k2885w

> Watch a video to learn about **Ancient Mesopotamia** at:
> https://www.youtube.com/watch?v=QeZKNjo-exs and/or
> https://www.youtube.com/watch?v=xVf5kZA0HtQ.

> Take a virtual tour to learn about the **Roman aqueducts** at:
> https://www.youtube.com/watch?v=v7N_uVBl17Y.

> Watch the documentary, **The Egtved Girl (2018),** about one of Denmark's most famous burial finds from the Bronze Age. It provides a glimpse into life in Europe of this early time. Available on Prime Videos.

> Watch the documentary, **The Lost Gardens of Babylon** (2014) in which Dr. Stephanie Dalley hunts for the mythical hanging gardens of Babylon. Available on Amazon Prime videos.

SMELTING

6,500 BCE

The Stone Age ended after people discovered metals. There's no set date when you can say we switched from one age to the next. The transition was slow and happened at different times around the world.

Like stones, metals are natural to the earth and can even be part of the stones themselves. Unlike stones, you can melt metals and mold them into something useful or pretty. The first metals discovered were gold, silver, copper, tin, and lead.

Smelting is a way to heat rocks to melt out the metals and remove any dirt so you can shape it. Humans learned to smelt lead around 6,500 BCE.

Mesopotamians were the first to mine and use copper between 8,000 and 5,000 B.C. The earliest artifacts using smelted copper are from 6,200 BCE. *Archeologists* also found evidence of copper mining in Michigan, North America, dating around 5,000 B.C. In 2020, archeologists discovered the oldest metal *furnace* found so far in Beersheba, Israel. It is from 4,000 BCE.

At first, the metals were a status symbol. People shaped it into jewelry and clothing ornaments. As they better understood how to mold and shape the metals, they started making more interesting things like statues and tools.

Copper is stronger than the other metals. People used it to make weapons, tools and other useful items — like swords and halberds, plows and axes, cauldrons and horns. Civilizations that had access to copper and knowledge of the smelting process had an advantage over those who didn't.

Copper was so important that we now call the brief time at the end of Stone Age, the "Copper Age."

The Copper Age lasted right up until someone discovered if you mix copper and tin together, you can make an even stronger metal. They called it *Bronze*. And thus began the Bronze Age and the science of *metallurgy*.

Learn more

- ➢ Read, *The Copper Age: When Metallurgy Came to Rule the World* from Ancient-Origins.net at: https://www.ancient-origins.net/artifacts-ancient-technology/copper-age-0015150

- ➢ Learn about the *Chalcolithic* period on Wikipedia at: https://en.wikipedia.org/wiki/Chalcolithic

- ➢ Read about the *Metals of Antiquity* from Wikipedia at: https://en.wikipedia.org/wiki/Metals_of_antiquity

- ➢ Read more about *Smelting* from Wikipedia at: https://en.wikipedia.org/wiki/Smelting

READING, WRITING, RESEARCH

Level 1

1. Gold artifacts are hard to find because people didn't just throw gold away. When an object was no longer useful, they melted it down to make something new. Today we call that recycling. Learn what metals and other materials can be recycled in our world today at: https://www.epa.gov/recycle/how-do-i-recycle-common-recyclables. Name five things that can be made with recycled materials.

2. Today, gold costs more than silver, copper, lead, or tin because gold stays pretty and doesn't *tarnish* or *corrode*. But in ancient times copper was the most valuable metal because it is stronger than the others. Set up a pretend store with different kinds of metal objects. Tell your customers why they should buy your copper items even though they cost more.

3. Before metals, people shaped rocks into tools and weapons like the hand axe, spear head, and arrow heads. Research and list three of the first tools or weapons that people made with copper. You can search online for "first copper tools" or "first copper weapons." Why do you think these metal items were better than rock?

4. Research and explain the difference between melting and smelting?

Level 2

1. Read *The Boy with the Bronze Axe* by Kathleen Fidler. Discuss what caused the conflict in the village when the boy presents his new ideas. Why do you think people reacted the way they did? How would you react to something new?

2. The Bronze Age ran from about 3,300 BCE to 1,200 BCE in the Near East, Mesopotamia and Egypt. Research to find out what life was like for people where you live during those years. Did they discover and use metals yet? Did they have cities and societies? What was their life like? As an added challenge, research also the area where your ancestors came from.

3. Read about the 6,500-year-old 'furnace' discovered in Beersheba at: https://www.jpost.com/archaeology/6500-year-old-furnace-in-beersheba-sheds-light-on-ancient-technology-644415. The article explains that refining copper was the "high-tech" of the time. It states that copper was not meant to be used by everyone. Who could use it and what did they do with it?

Level 3

1. Elements are generally classified as metals, nonmetals, and metalloids. Review the periodic table and make a list of all the elements that are metals. Research the properties of each. Indicate (yes or no) if it's possible to shape each elemental metal into an artifact. How many of those shapeable metals were in use during the Bronze Age? Of those that were not, research to find out when each was discovered and explain its first use after discovery.

2. Research the melting points of each of the Bronze Age metals. Find out and explain how the ancient people were able to get a fire hot enough to melt the metals. How did they separate out dirt and other impurities?

3. Stone Age humans used their weapons for hunting meat, not fighting wars. Research and explain what changed between the Stone Age and Bronze Age that made men turn their weapons on each other.

STEAM ACTIVITIES AND MORE

Level 1

1. Visit a museum and look for metal artifacts from ancient civilizations like Egypt, Mesopotamia, China, or Peru. Talk about the metal objects and what they were used for. Pick your favorite and tell someone about why you like it.

2. Search "Keep it cool, make it melt" video on YouTube and learn how to melt solids using heat and chocolate.

3. Melt crayons together to form new colors: Use blue and yellow to make green; blue and red to make purple; red and yellow to make orange. Bronze is made from mixing copper and tin. Do you have crayons in those colors? As an alternative, you can mix food coloring in white icing, or mix different colored gelatin. Talk about why mixing two colors makes a new color.

Level 2

1. Visit a museum and look for metal artifacts from ancient civilizations like Egypt, Mesopotamia, China, or Peru. Pick your favorite and research it to learn more. When was it made? Who made it? What is it used for? Who found it? Where was it found and why do you think it was preserved?

2. Learn the craft of copper rubbing and create your own design. Frame your work when you're done. Watch one of these videos or research your own: https://www.youtube.com/watch?v=PcGRPSFm0KU or https://www.youtube.com/watch?v=GUOcdEgoCqE.
Safety tip: have an adult tape the raw edges of the copper before you work with it because it is sharp!

3. Gallium is a soft metal with a low melting temperature. In fact, hot water will melt it. Search on "DIY metal melting experiment for kids" or watch the video at: https://www.kidzsearch.com/kidztube/making-melting-metal-at-home-science-experiments-you-can-do-at-home-lab-360_0b1850a16.html. You can buy gallium online and use it to melt and remold into a coin or trinket.

Level 3

1. Make a candle from a mold. Fill a shallow box with damp, packable sand and level it off. Choose an object that you want to replicate as a candle. Depress it halfway into the sand and pull it out. Then flip the object over and depress it into another section of sand. You should have two opposite-side molds of the same object. Melt soy, bees, or paraffin wax in a double boiler. If desired, add wax coloring or shaved crayons. Fill your two molds with the melted wax. After the two halves are hardened, you'll need to add a wick. Heat the flat side of each candle half with a blow dryer so it begins to melt. Lay the wick on one half so it will sticks out the top Then press the two halves together and allow them to re-harden as one unit.

2. Research how to make a forge. Write a report about how a forge works. If you have the equipment and a willing parent, you can attempt to build a backyard forge. Research your own or visit this website for homemade forge ideas: https://www.thefamilyhomestead.com/homemade-forge-plans-tutorials-for-every-skill-level/

COLORING PAGE

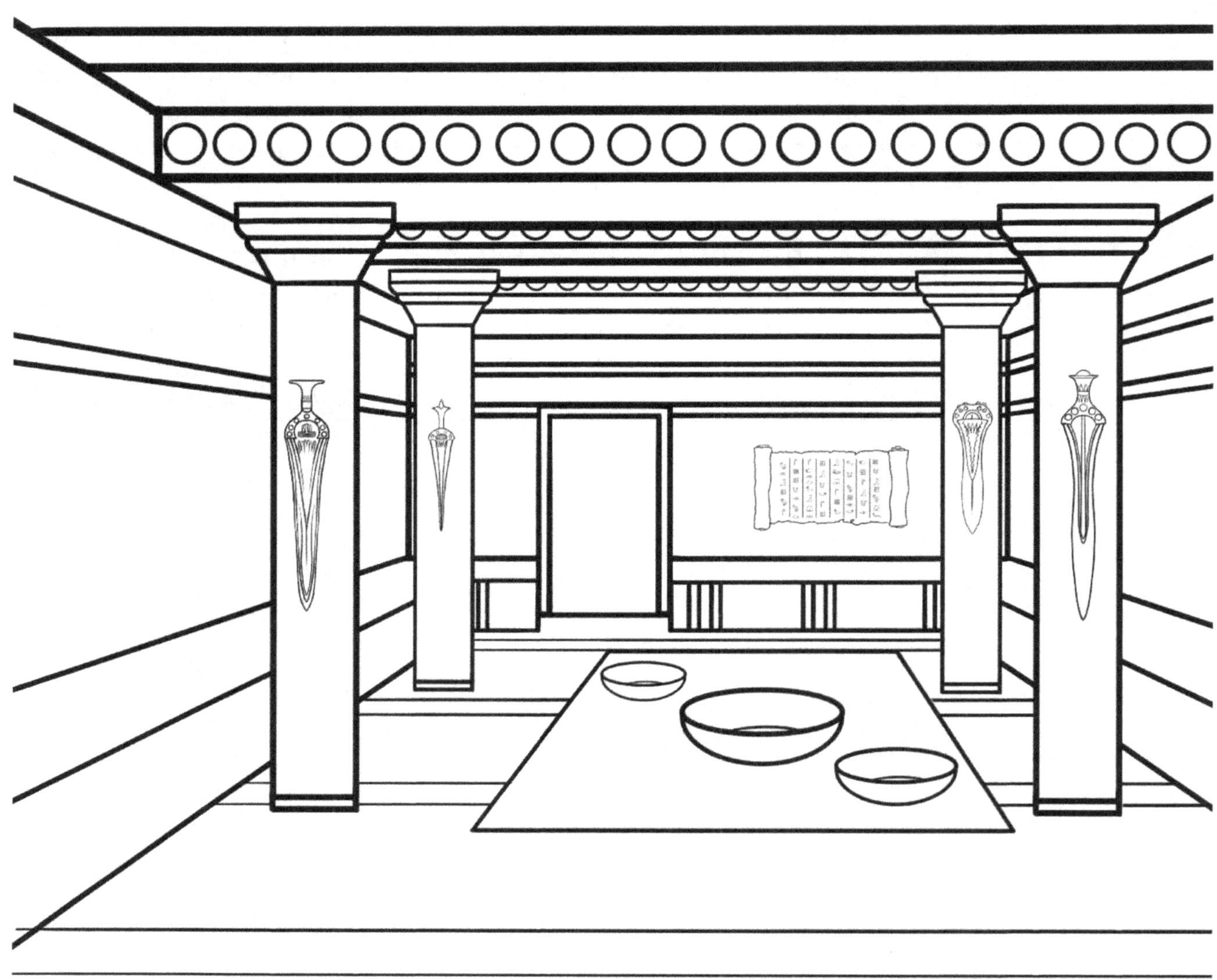

WORD SEARCH

Find these terms in the puzzle:

Alloy	Chalcolithic	Halberd	Shields
Armor	Copper	Impurities	Slag
Bellows	Forge	Mining	Smelting
Bronze Age	Furnace	Mold	Swords
Caldron	Gallium	Plow	Weaponry

INVENTION DISCUSSION PAGE

Name:____Date:________________

Invention/Product:____

Who invented it?____When?___________

How does it work?

____

____

____

What problem did it solve?

____

____

____

What was it like before the product was invented? What did people use or do instead?

____

____

____

Who could own it? (Did everyone get to use it? Was it expensive? Was it easy to get?)

____

____

____

Can anyone use this product? What skill was needed to operate it?

____

____

____

Is the product still in use today? How has it changed since its original invention?

____

____

____

IRRIGATION

6,000 BCE

The agricultural revolution ended the way of life for Stone Age hunter-gatherers. People settled near rivers to become farmers instead. Small villages soon grew into towns and cities.

Mesopotamia was the first civilization with cities. It was located between the Tigris and Euphrates rivers. Mesopotamia in Greek means "land between the rivers."

As the population grew, people started to move farther away from the rivers. But they had to run back and forth from the river to get water for their crops. They needed a better way to get the water from the river to their farms.

Someone thought to dig a long trench from the river. The water would flow along this *canal* from the river all the way to the farm. We call this *irrigation*. They built a wooden door in the canal to open when they needed water, and close when they had enough.

Canal irrigation was used as far back as 6,000 BCE in the Jordan Valley. Irrigation took many forms over the years. The Minoan civilization on Crete used clay pipe *aqueducts* in the early 2nd millennium.

By 300 BCE, the Romans built sophisticated systems to catch melting snow from the Alps. They used *tunnels*, canals, *clay pipes*, and even *bridges* to bring the water out of the mountains and to their fields, cities, *bath houses*, and *drinking fountains*.

Learn more

> ➢ Take a virtual tour to learn about the ***Roman aqueducts*** at:
> https://www.youtube.com/watch?v=v7N_uVBl17Y.

> ➢ Read about ***Irrigation*** from Kids Britannica at:
> https://kids.britannica.com/kids/article/irrigation/353304

> ➢ Read ***Irrigation: An historical perspective*** by Sojka, Robert E., David L. Bjorneberg and James A. Entry (2005), available at:
> https://eprints.nwisrl.ars.usda.gov/id/eprint/815/1/1070.pdf.

- ➤ Read *Irrigation in Mesopotamia* in the World History Encyclopedia at: https://www.worldhistory.org/video/1102/irrigation-in-mesopotamia/.

- ➤ Read *Aqueduct* in the World History Encyclopedia at: https://www.worldhistory.org/aqueduct/.

READING, WRITING, RESEARCH

Level 1

1. Look on an Atlas to find big cities that are old, like Paris, London and Rome. Why do you think these cities are all close to water?

2. Look up a map of ancient Mesopotamia. The word Mesopotamia means "land between the rivers." Why do you think the hunter-gatherers settled here first? Besides water, what else made it a good place for farming?

3. Take a family drive in the country and look for signs of irrigation. What does it look like? How does it differ from Ancient forms of irrigation?

Level 2

1. Learn some new vocabulary. Look up the meaning of: *nilometer*, *shadoof*, and *sakieh.* Write the definitions and explain how each helped ancient Egyptians. Learn how to pronounce each word properly.

2. While irrigation brought water to farm crops in ancient times, how did the people get drinking water? Research online for, "how did Bronze Age people get drinking water"?

3. Read about how people in ancient times filtered water at: https://askdruniverse.wsu.edu/2018/08/31/dr-universe-people-ancient-times-filter-water/. Name three ways to clean the dirty water.

Level 3

1. Take a virtual tour to learn about the Roman aqueducts at https://www.youtube.com/watch?v=v7N_uVBI17Y. You can also learn how aqueducts work at https://www.youtube.com/watch?v=xGM1rsnbpE4. What was the Roman aqueduct made from? How did they keep the aqueducts clean? How did the water continue flowing even though the ground was uneven?

2. Learn about ancient Greek cisterns at: https://www.thecivilengineer.org/education/online-historical-database-of-civil-infrastructure/ancient-greek-cisterns. When was the cistern first invented? What different methods were used to get water into the cistern? Besides the cistern, were the other two primary water supply sources for ancient Greeks?

3. Hunter-gatherers were fairly safe from water-borne illnesses. Living in cities created a demand for water sources, but also increased the likelihood of contamination. Pure water became an early priority. How did these ancient people purify their water?

STEAM ACTIVITIES AND MORE

Level 1

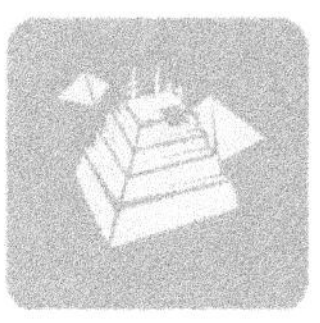 

1. If you have access, go to a beach and build a sandcastle. Then create an irrigation channel to bring sea water to your moat. Think about the water level and how deep you must dig your trench to get the water to the shore. As an alternative, make a small model at home in a sandbox, fish tank or plastic tub.

2. Visit https://www.sciencebuddies.org/stem-activities/build-an-irrigation-system or search on "build an irrigation system" to learn how to make one using paper cups and straws.

3. Draw a picture of an ancient town with a river, a field and a canal. Share with someone and explain how the canal worked.

Level 2

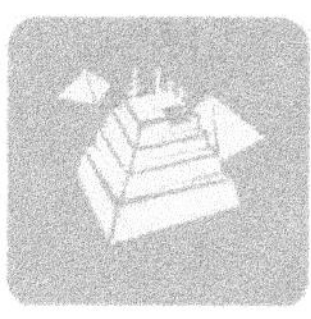

1. Search on "Easy STEAM irrigation system" for instructions to make an irrigation model in a baking pan.

2. Make a model of a shadoof using sticks, string, stones and other simple items.

3. Learn how to remove dirt and impurities from water at https://kids.nationalgeographic.com/books/article/water-wonders. Then try it!!

Level 3

1. Build a model aqueduct out of craft supplies. For added challenge, build a real one in your yard. Take it from a water hose, spigot or other outdoor water source to a garden or other need for water.

2. Build a water filtration system. Learn how at: https://www.homesciencetools.com/article/water-filtration-science-project//

3. Watch a video to learn how math helps to save lives when it comes to safe drinking water. https://newmfgalliance.org/get_real_math_video/what-does-clean-drinking-water-have-to-do-with-math/. You can also download the Lesson Plan from the website and work with your math teacher to complete the lesson.

IRRIGATION SYSTEM

Which of the cups will fill first? Which cup will fill up last? Why?

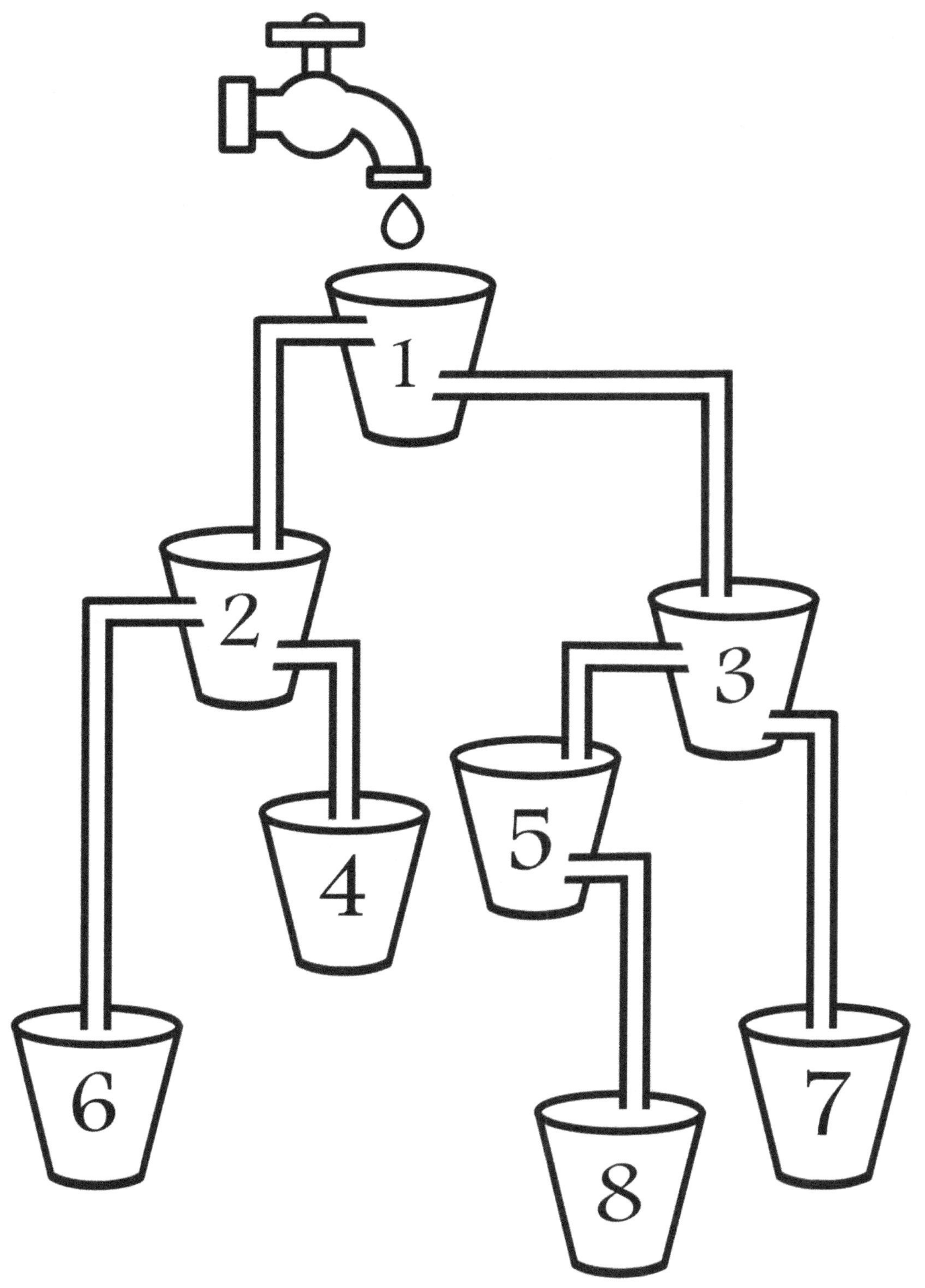

CROSSWORD PUZZLE

Across:

1 Artificial waterways for irrigation

5 A pipe or conduit for bringing water from a distant source

7 To supply land with water

8 An overflow of water in a land normally dry

9 A large stream of water that flows into an ocean or lake

10 Prolonged dry weather

Down:

2 Helped Ancient Egyptians predict flood levels of the Nile

3 Pole and bucket method of watering crops

4 A place where water is collected and stored for later use

6 A water wheel used by Ancient Egyptians

10 A barrier built to hold back flowing water

INVENTION DISCUSSION PAGE

Name:____Date:______________________

Invention/Product:____

Who invented it?____When?_____________

How does it work?

____

____

____

What problem did it solve?

____

____

____

What was it like before the product was invented? What did people use or do instead?

____

____

____

Who could own it? (Did everyone get to use it? Was it expensive? Was it easy to get?)

____

____

____

Can anyone use this product? What skill was needed to operate it?

____

____

____

Is the product still in use today? How has it changed since its original invention?

____

____

____

BOATS

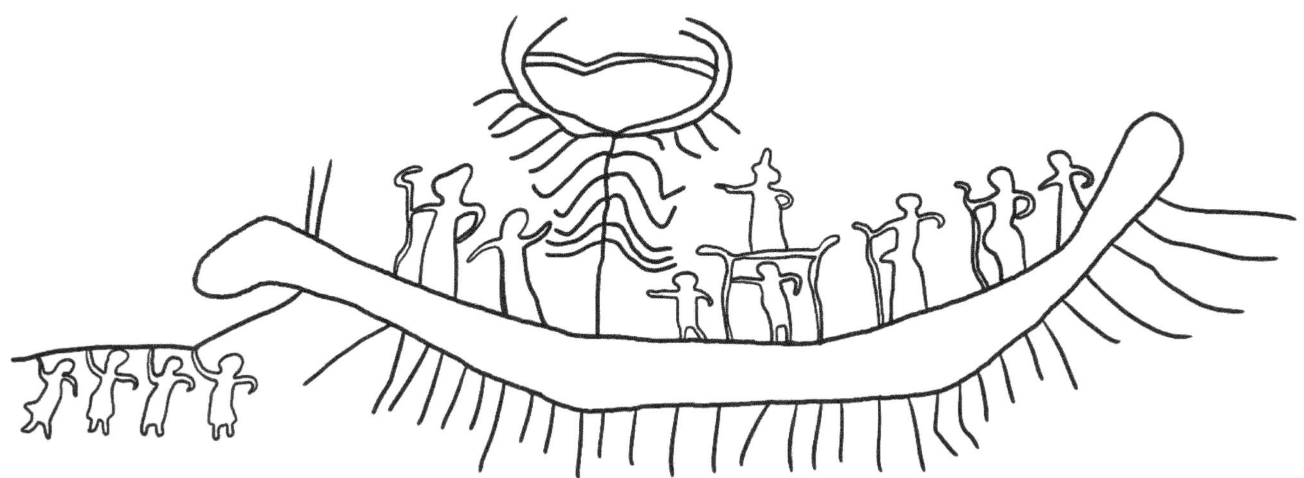

Reproduction petroglyph of Aswan boat carrying an early Pharoah.

As soon as humans noticed that logs could float, there was the potential for making rafts and canoes. But trees rot and become soil over time. They wouldn't leave traces for us to find. We may never know the true age of boating.

But, there are some clues. A 12,000 year old rock carving in Azerbaijan shows a *boat* made of reeds. The oldest *canoe* found so far is from Holland dated about 10,000 years ago.

Floating down a river on a log is not the same as sailing a boat across the sea. A boat takes a lot more engineering. Scientists believe *sea-worthy* boats have been around a very long time. How else could humans make it to Australia 50,000 years ago? But that evidence has yet to be found.

The oldest sea-worthy *watercraft* we know of are from the early Bronze Age's *Ubaid* period. That is the term given to the Tell al-'Ubaid excavation site that spanned 5,500 – 4,200 BCE. Ubaid boats helped early Mesopotamians *transport* goods up and down the Euphrates and Tigris rivers.

We know their boats were sea-worthy because Ubaidian pottery has been found all around the Persian Gulf. That shows their trade went far beyond the rivers.

Ancient ceramic Ubaid boat models show us what they looked like. They were small, canoe-shaped boats with a *mast* and an upturned *bow*. The small size of the boats tells us the trade business was small.

They may have traded food and other perishable goods for *bitumen*, which is a type of asphalt they used to repair their boats. Ubaidians also traded for copper and semi-precious stones like lapis lazuli and turquoise.

Boats were equally important to Egyptians who lived on the Nile in 4,000 BCE. Their artwork shows boats made of lashed together reeds with poles and *sails*. Once they developed carpentry around 3,500 BCE, they started making boats out of wood.

The Egyptians traded with people around the Red Sea, Mediterranean and other places on the Nile. They sent out papyrus, pottery, and perfume and brought back turquoise, spices, frankincense, copper, iron, and tin.

There is another civilization that used boats. Many ancient texts mention battles with a war-like people from the sea. But, none of the texts say where the Sea People came from or the kinds of boats they used.

There is still a lot of mystery about ancient boats and much more yet to discover.

Learn more

➢ Read how **Mesopotamian Reed Boats Changed the Stone Age** from Thoughco at: https://www.thoughtco.com/mesopotamian-reed-boats-171674.

➢ Read about the world's oldest boat, the ***Pesse canoe*** from Ancient-origins.net at: https://www.ancient-origins.net/artifacts-ancient-technology/pesse-canoe-0017298.

➢ Read about the mysterious "Sea people" in the World History Encyclopedia at: https://www.worldhistory.org/Sea_Peoples/

READING, WRITING, RESEARCH

Level 1

1. Ancient Egyptian boats were made of papyrus. How is that possible? How could it stay afloat? Hint: You might find an answer in the Papyrus, Parchment and Paper section of this book!

2. Look up a picture of the world's oldest boat and then draw it. What kind of boat was it? How many people could it hold? How do you think they steered it?

3. Other parts were later added to help move and steer the boat. Look up these boating terms and learn about them: Sail, tiller, rudder, mast.

4. Read <u>We're Sailing Down the Nile: A Journey Through Egypt</u> by Laurie Krebs (for ages 4 to 7). What kind of boat are they using? Was that a real boat in ancient Egypt? Are the people in the boat from old times or new times? How can you tell? Do the people in the story sail past old places or new places?

Level 2

1. Review the timeline of boats at: <u>https://illuminatingfacts.com/timeline-of-boats/</u>. How many different uses for ancient boats can you name? Do we still use them for the same purposes? Do we have additional purposes or fewer?

2. Learn about the mysterious "Sea People" and tell where you think they may have come from. Why do you think that?

3. Scientists believe people traveled to the Americas over 20,000 years ago. How do you think they get here? Research to find out if you're right.

Level 3

1. Research the Ubaid period of Mesopotamia and describe its civilizations.

2. One invention often leads to others. Consider the needs of a boat on the sea and name as many other inventions that likely stemmed from it. Hint: think beyond parts of a boat. What new necessities might boating have caused?

3. Research the Mesopotamian trade routes. Then measure the furthest these early civilizations had to travel to make their trades. How long would it take to make the round trip from start to finish in their type of boat?

STEAM ACTIVITIES AND MORE

Level 1

1. Play "Sink or Float." You'll need a tub or tank of water, plus objects and toys from around the house. Decide up front if you think each object will sink in the water or float on top. What are the differences between those that sank versus those that floated? For example, what are the shapes? What are they made from? Are they solid or hollow? Tell somebody which floats best.

2. Create a raft out of craft sticks. Decide how to propel it. Will it use oars or a sail? For ideas, you can search online for "craft stick raft."

3. Find three ways to make a boat out of trash, recyclables or toys. Search online or on Pinterest for inspiration, if needed.

Level 2

1. Using a sheet of craft foam (like construction paper, but made of foam) draw and cut out different size rectangular "rafts" – small, medium and large. Float all your foam rafts in a tub. Then one-by-one, add pennies to each raft. Use the same amount of weights on each raft. Which one do you think will sink first? Why?

Next make different sized boats using heavy or double-layered aluminum foil. Make sure your boats have sides so water cannot get in. Do the same penny experiment to see if they can hold more or less weight before sinking.

2. Learn about surface tension at: https://www.khanacademy.org/science/physics/fluids/fluid-dynamics/v/surface-tension-and-adhesion. Then try a trick with the foam rafts you made in Level 2, #1. Snip one end of your rectangular raft to form a pointed front. At the other end, cut out a tiny notch to represent where a motor might be attached. Float your revised "boat." Then put a drop of dish soap into the notch at the back. What happens when you break the surface tension with the dish soap? Why?

3. Add a sail to your aluminum foil boats. You can use more aluminum foil to fashion your mast and sail. Or visit https://inspirationlaboratories.com/how-to-build-a-boat/ for other sail boat ideas. Then have a sailboat race with someone else. More sail will catch more wind. Try to improve your boat to go faster.

Level 3

1. Make a small raft using materials you find in nature, just large enough to hold some rocks. If possible, find a safe water source to float your raft. [As an alternative, make a raft model out craft sticks and float it in a tub of water.] Add weight to your raft. How much weight can your raft hold? What can you do to make your raft hold more weight?

2. Archimedes was a famous mathematician and inventor from ancient Greece. The *Archimedes' Principle* has to do with buoyancy of objects and displacement when you place them in a fluid. Learn about the Archimedes Principle and try the lesson/experiments at: https://www.khanacademy.org/science/physics/fluids/buoyant-force-and-archimedes-principle/a/buoyant-force-and-archimedes-principle-article or https://www.teachengineering.org/activities/view/wsu_eureka_activity.

WORD SEARCH

```
S U R F A C E T E N S I O N W N Z
Z E D Z N A Y I M L M D N Y T V U
Q Y T P X A M O U I L Y Y X T M F
K C E A P Y E T K Z I J W N B W O
D N H T R W R N K X A P D T P T E
I A L L U H A E A R S F I P S J L
S Y E K X O P T V R E J C A W T P
P O S O D N R U E I R D M K G T O
L U T V N Q I E E R R E D J S K E
A B I N F A M L D Q C S T U C B P
C T L V C L C O E A P R I I R N A
E V L P G I O E V H R B A R D R E
M B E W D W D A S T B T C F G E S
E M R T S T Y F T S T L N X T I M
N K I R A F T J L R E E D B O A T
T F L U G N A I S R E P R R Z G E
U B A I D I A N P O T T E R Y A A
```

Buoyancy	Mediterranean	Reed Boat	Tigris River
Displacement	Nile	Rudder	Tiller
Euphrates	Persian Gulf	Sail	Trade Route
Float	Pesse Canoe	Sea People	Ubaidian Pottery
Mast	Raft	Surface tension	Watercraft

MAZE

Find your way from the top of the mast to the bottom of the hull and out into the sea.

INVENTION DISCUSSION PAGE

Name:____Date:_________________________

Invention/Product:____

Who invented it?____When?________________

How does it work?

____

____

____

What problem did it solve?

____

____

____

What was it like before the product was invented? What did people use or do instead?

____

____

____

Who could own it? (Did everyone get to use it? Was it expensive? Was it easy to get?)

____

____

____

Can anyone use this product? What skill was needed to operate it?

____

____

____

Is the product still in use today? How has it changed since its original invention?

____

____

____

ROPE

4,000 BCE

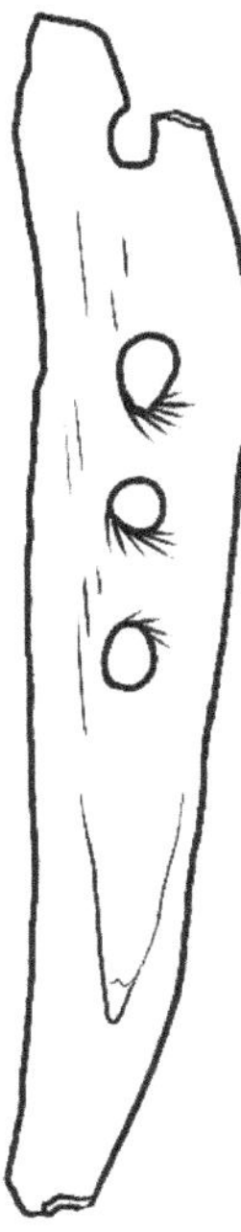

Earliest man would have used vines, long grasses and other natural materials to tie things. These weren't strong enough for heavier uses like climbing or pulling an animal carcass. But it got people thinking.

Soon someone twisted a few strands and discovered it made their grass stronger. Eureka! Rope was born! At least that's one possibility.

Recent discoveries show that hunter-gatherers had a simple tool for making *rope* and *twine* as far back as 40,000 years. The tool was carved from *ivory* with holes for twisting the fibers. Twine could better help them climb, cross rivers, tie clothing and secure possessions.

Around 4,000 BCE, the Egyptians made a stronger rope out of water reed *fibers*. They also learned how to mass produce it. Lucky for us, they recorded how they made their rope. They needed a lot of rope for huge projects like building the pyramids. They later invented a *pulley* system that used rope to hoist buckets of water out of a well.

The Chinese made rope from *hemp* around 2,800 BCE. The craft of rope-making also spread west into Europe.

From building monuments and sailing across the sea to reining in animals, rope was a handy thing to have around during the Bronze Age. Professional rope makers had a secure job.

Learn more

➢ Read ***The Invention of Rope*** from Rope and Cord at:
https://ropeandcord.com/guides-ideas/the-invention-of-rope/.

➢ Read ***How rope was made 40,000 years ago*** from Science Daily at:
www.sciencedaily.com/releases/2016/07/160722093459.htm.

READING, WRITING, RESEARCH

Level 1

1. What do you think was the first "necessity" that inspired hunter-gatherers to invent rope? Why did the Egyptians feel the need to improve rope? And why did they need so much of it?

2. Read about the invention of rope at https://ropeandcord.com/guides-ideas/the-invention-of-rope/. How many people did it take to make the rope in ancient Egypt?

3. Search online to find and watch a video on "how to make rope" or visit https://www.youtube.com/watch?v=thDYZ3tzUN8. If rope can coil, explain why the room where rope is made is so long.

Level 2

1. Basic knots include: Figure 8, overhand, sheet bend, half knot, square knot, and slip knot. Look up and explain what purpose each is used for.

2. Read about boats on page 29. Do you think sailboats could have been invented before rope? Why or why not?

3. The *pulley* is a simple machine. Research how it works and explain it to someone in your family.

Level 3

1. Research available plant and animal fibers from around the world during the Bronze Age. What could they have used to make rope in Africa, Asia, Europe and the Near East where different climates would produce different resources?

2. When did each of the major civilizations start making and using rope? Which ones invented it and which ones adopted it after seeing it from travelers?

3. How does rope and rope making differ today than from ancient times? Are today's ropes stronger or the same as ancient ropes? What are they made of?

STEAM ACTIVITIES AND MORE

Level 1

1. Wrap clothesline, rope or twine around something useful, like a pencil holder or planter to decorate it. Secure with glue and paint or color your project with markers.

2. Make the perfect size jump rope: Measure your height from armpit to ground. Multiply by two. That's how long the main part of the rope should be. Add an extra twelve inches to make a knot at both ends or to wrap around your hands.

3. Play tug of war with two teams. Use one rope with knots tied at various lengths and the other rope with no knots. How did the knots make a difference? Discuss with your team which rope was best and why.

4. Visit https://tinkergarten.com/activities/pulley-play or https://carrotsareorange.com/how-to-make-a-pulley/ to learn how pulleys work. Make one for yourself!

Level 2

1. To make rope, you need fibers to twist into yarn, yarn to twist into strands, and strands to twist into rope. Try making your own rope by hand twisting strings of thread. Then create a tool using heavy cardboard like the one the hunter-gatherers had. Discuss the difference in difficulty and time involved between hand twisting and using the tool. (Visit https://www.ibtimes.co.uk/mammoth-ivory-tool-40000-years-ago-solves-puzzle-how-our-ancestors-made-rope-1572597 to learn about the tool.)

2 Make something useful out of twine or clothesline. Get ideas from Pinterest or other online craft sites.

3. Practice making each of these basic knots: Figure 8, overhand, sheet bend, half knot, square knot, and slip knot.

Level 3

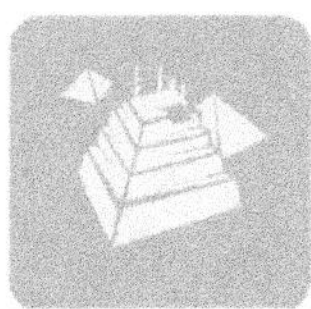

1. Imagine you live in ancient Babylon. You have a garden that hangs high on a wall and those plants get thirsty during the dry season. Invent a pulley system to get water up to them. Search online for instructions if you need help.

2. Test to see which size jump rope helps you jump fastest. Buy (or make from clothesline) a 10-foot jump rope. Using a stop watch in 1-minute tests, count the number of jumps you can make with different lengths of rope. Start with ten feet, then adjust the size by making slip knots in the ends. Measure and record the size and number of jumps, until the rope is too short to jump. Which length was fastest?

KNOT MATCH

Draw a line from each knot to its name.

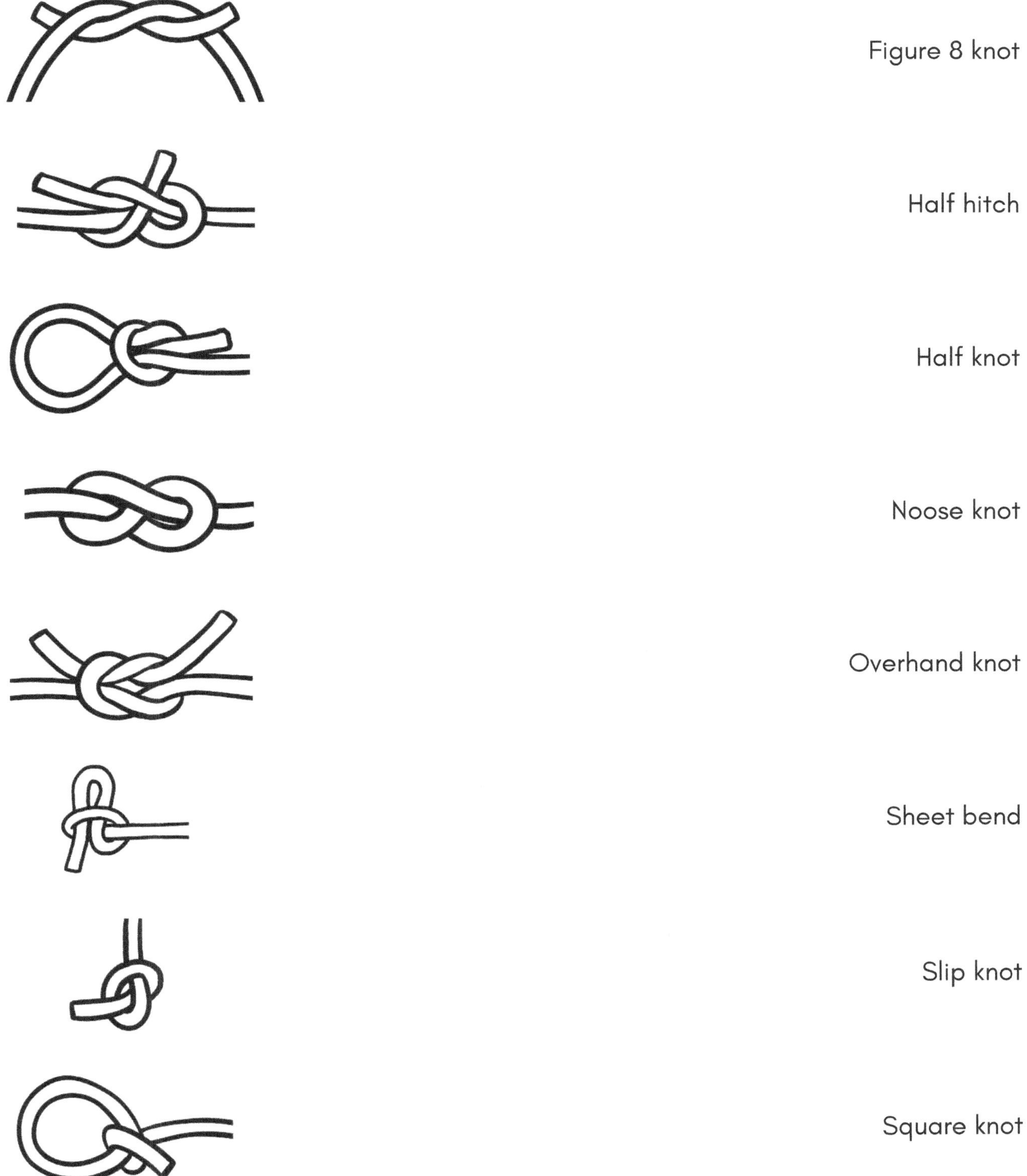

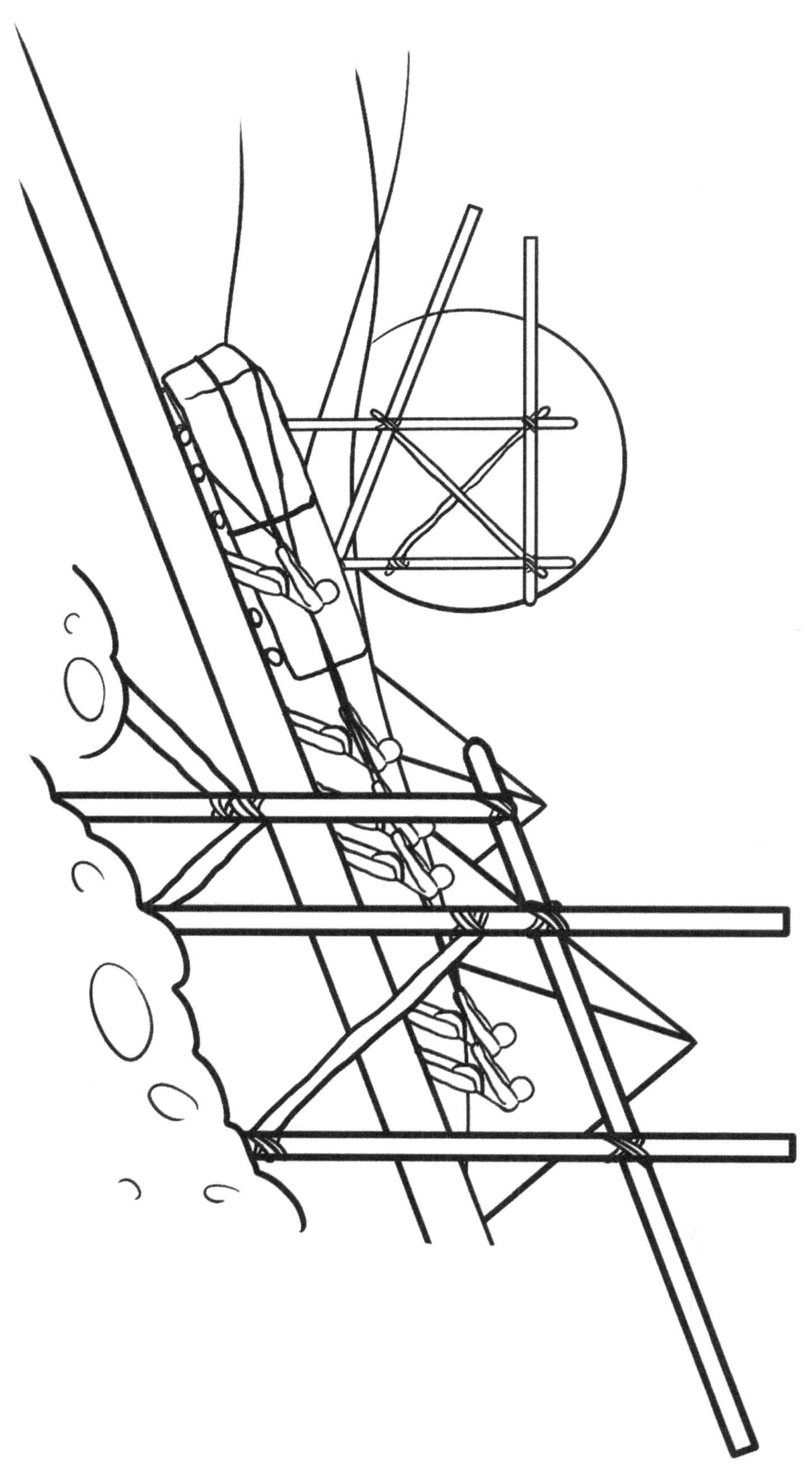

INVENTION DISCUSSION PAGE

Name:____Date:_________________

Invention/Product:____

Who invented it?_____________________________________When?_______________

How does it work?

____

____

____

What problem did it solve?

____

____

____

What was it like before the product was invented? What did people use or do instead?

____

____

____

Who could own it? (Did everyone get to use it? Was it expensive? Was it easy to get?)

____

____

____

Can anyone use this product? What skill was needed to operate it?

____

____

____

Is the product still in use today? How has it changed since its original invention?

____

____

____

PAPYRUS, PARCHMENT, PAPER

3,200 BCE

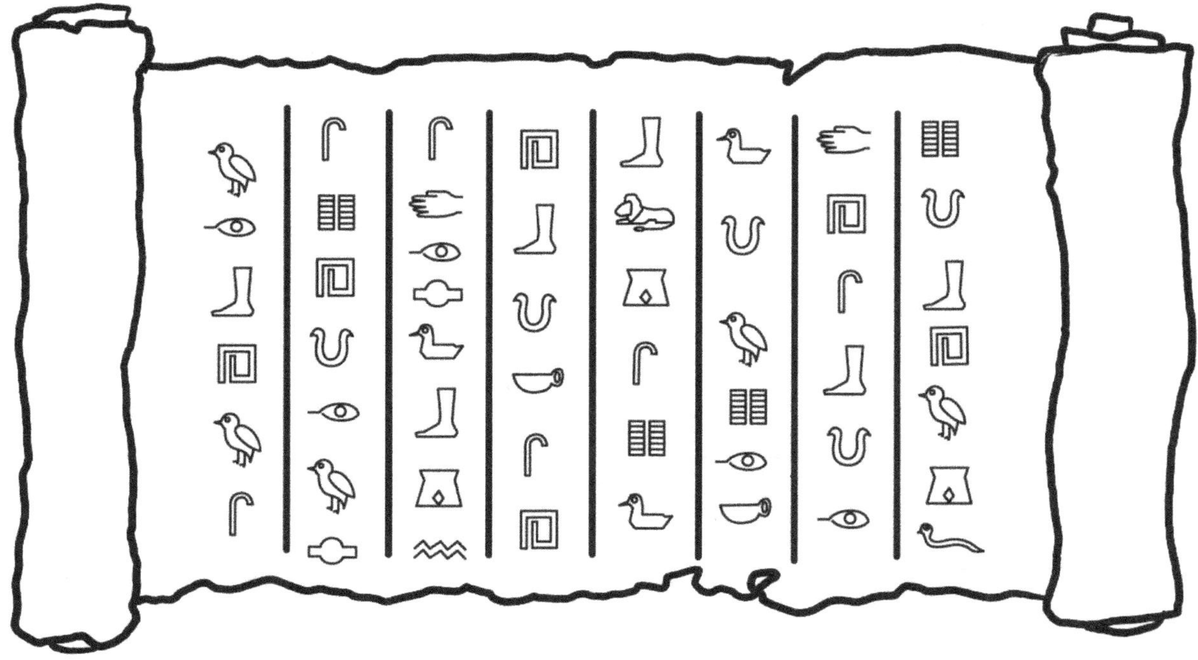

The first written *communications* were chiseled into rocks. That was tedious work! So the Egyptians found a better way. They started to write on *papyrus*, possibly as early as the 3,200 BCE.

Papyrus is a plant that used to grow in vast amounts in the Nile river valley. It grows in stalks sometimes up to 16 feet high. Since it's a plant that floats, early Egyptians used papyrus *reeds* to make their boats.

They didn't just pick papyrus leaves and start writing. They had to cut open the *stalks* and use the *pith*. That's the soft spongy part inside the stalk. They cut the pith into strips and laid them side by side. Then they put another layer across it sideways. Papyrus is the term used for the plant, but it is also the term used for the resulting writing material.

The Latin word papyrus means, "paper made of papyrus stalks." The Greek word papyros means, "any plant of the paper plant genus." Both words stem from the Egyptian word for papyrus. Our word for *paper* also comes from the root word of papyrus.

While Egyptians were writing on papyrus, the Chinese were writing on *bamboo*. In Asia Minor, they were writing on animal skins. They would have seen papyrus on their trade routes and came up with their own ideas. *Parchment* was made from sheep skin and *vellum* was made from calf skin. Both were invented around 1,500 BCE.

The Chinese are the ones who invented *paper* like we know today. They first made it during the Han dynasty (202 BCE – 220 AD/CE) in the Iron Age.

Once you have something to write on, you could record anything. People wrote lists of their possessions and things they sold. Other people wrote about things that were important to them. The oldest *books* were written on *scrolls* and date back to 4,000 BCE!

Learn more

➢ Read *Egyptian Papyrus* at WorldHistory.org at:
https://www.worldhistory.org/Egyptian_Papyrus/.

➢ Read *The Three P's: Papyrus, Parchment and Paper* from the University of Adelaide at: https://www.adelaide.edu.au/library/special/exhibitions/cover-to-cover/papyrus/.

READING, WRITING, RESEARCH

Level 1

1. Visit a local museum and look for items made of papyrus or parchment. Choose one to learn about it. How well was it preserved? What is its condition? Find out where it was discovered and what information is on it.

2. Take a virtual tour of the Papyrus Museum in Austria. Link to it at https://www.onb.ac.at/en/museums/papyrus-museum/about-the-papyrus-museum/virtual-papyrus-museum. Write about the three most interesting things you saw or learned.

3. Visit https://artsandculture.google.com/story/a-brief-history-of-books/OAXR-SPrQmOCew?hl=en to learn about the history of books. What does the oldest book look like? What is it about?

Level 2

1. Besides writing material, research to learn what other uses the ancient Egyptians had for papyrus. List as many as you can.

2. Research to find out what the Egyptians used to write with. Hint; it wasn't a quill! What did they use for ink? Next research what the Chinese used for pen and ink and discuss how it differs from the Egyptians.

3. Research vellum and explain how it is different from parchment and papyrus.

4. Chinese invented paper a thousand years after the Bronze Age ended. But they didn't use paper for writing. Research to find out what they did with their paper.

Level 3

1. Research and write about the oldest known library in the world and what it contained.

2. What is the origin of the word *Codex*? What is the difference between the words, *library* and *bibliotheca*?

3. Research online or visit a museum to learn how professionals care for historic documents. How do they keep the documents from the damage caused by age and handling?

4. Just as today, the quality of paper from antiquity can vary depending on who manufactured it and how. The durability of the paper also depends on how it is stored over time. When ancient people recorded events that happened, those sheets of papyrus, parchment or even paper eventually will have started to disintegrate. Someone would have to recopy those older essays or lose them forever. Consider and explain how that might affect our understanding of ancient historical events today.

STEAM ACTIVITIES AND MORE

Level 1

1. Did you know a page in a book is called a 'leaf"? Take a walk around your neighborhood and look for the largest leaf you can find. Collect several of them. Then take them home and write about the invention of paper on them. Bind your leaf pages into a book.

2. Make your own papyrus with untreated parchment paper (from an office store) or brown paper bag. Make a solution of 2 cups water and 1 cup flour. Then cut your paper into strips about 1 ½ to 2 inches wide and soak them in the flour mixture. Pull the strips out one at a time and lay them side by side on a clean surface. Each one should just overlap the next at the edges. Then lay a second row in the sideways direction on top of the first. Cover with tin foil and use a rolling pin to smooth out your wet papyrus. Remove the foil and let it dry.

3. Write a story or practice writing hieroglyphics on your homemade papyrus.

Level 2

1. Make recycled paper: Search methods online or find three ways to do it at: https://www.wikihow.com/Make-Recycled-Paper.

2. Look up and learn the art of origami. Try to make three different things using the techniques.

3. Use the methods above to make either papyrus or recycled paper and create a scroll. Write about the invention of paper on your scroll. Then share your story with someone who will appreciate it.

Level 3

1. Use the methods above to make either papyrus or recycled paper and create a scroll. Develop a method to preserve your homemade paper.

2. Learn the science behind the Vesuvius challenge of resurrecting an ancient library from the ashes of a volcano. Visit https://scrollprize.org/ or look up 'Herculaneum Papyri, Dr. Brent Seales, University of Kentucky" and watch the drama unfold.

WORD SEARCH

```
U S L M V N T B G N K R U J Z C B W I V K
F T E N O B K I S E T E V T H U G I D M Y
C D W X B O I B B J H P Z Z F O I W S N P
V I W S O L R L N W S A D D D A G E U G D
A S E B C L Z I E A R P V E Z K C M R B O
Y I X E D O C O P A D I Q E L L O B Y W U
K N J Q C R F T D V A P T W Y C K F P D A
K T S Q J C E H E F J C O I N C Y Y A M H
Y E Q C A S D E E F Q Y N P N I I C P I F
S G Z Q E N C C R P U P M D V G F J E W O
J R K L H N N A W R T B P T U M L X Q R E
C A L F S K I N M E U O K D T K R W I A T
O T N W V M K X B S D N R K T B Z G B G D
A E F Q S N S T N E M H C R A P A M B E E
W F Z P R J P W R R L L S R O M T E G M D
J M U R K S E C S V B S E S I M J I T S S
O F A E L A E Z U E F G A Z T F X V N B Y
R M G W X D H C O M M U N I C A T I O N O
V M E J A Z S Y U J A Q Q V T I H C G Q D
M U L L E V N I L E R I V E R V A L L E Y
L I B R A R Y O F A S H U R B A N I P A L
```

Bibliotheca	Disintegrate	Paper	Reed pen
Book	Leaf	Papyrus	Scroll
Calfskin	Library of Ashurbanipal	Parchment	Sheepskin
Codex	Nile River Valley	Preserve	Vellum
Communication	Origami	Recycle	Writing

COLORING PAGE

INVENTION DISCUSSION PAGE

Name:____Date:________________

Invention/Product:____

Who invented it?____When?_______________

How does it work?

____

____

____

What problem did it solve?

____

____

____

What was it like before the product was invented? What did people use or do instead?

____

____

____

Who could own it? (Did everyone get to use it? Was it expensive? Was it easy to get?)

____

____

____

Can anyone use this product? What skill was needed to operate it?

____

____

____

Is the product still in use today? How has it changed since its original invention?

____

____

____

SOAP

2,800 BCE

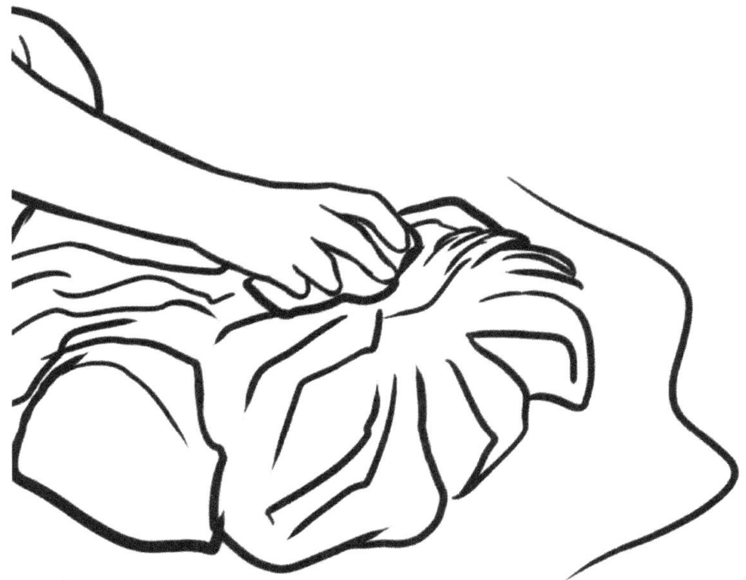

a *cleaning agent* to wash their greasy became one of the key ingredients of

erian was the first to produce soap he same time the Egyptians were ding the Great Pyramid of Giza. merian writings say they used *resin* om fir trees. The Babylonians and yptians then created new recipes sing plant ash, oils, and animal fat.

The earliest mention of soap is from a cuneiform tablet about washing the *lanolin* fats from wool in the textile industry. Another Sumerian text explains that soap was used to help a person with a skin condition – like a *lotion*. And it worked! Probably because they washed away the bacteria that caused the rash.

Later they used soap for washing clothes, floors, dishes and other obviously dirty objects. They only used soap to wash dirty objects. If something looked clean, there was no need to wash it.

No one thought to bathe with soap. They didn't understand germs yet. When people's bodies were dirty, they bathed in the river using the sand or silt as a scrub. Many simply used water to wash away dirt and grime. When they felt clean, they applied scented olive oil to their skin, which they had to scrape off using a tool called a *strigel*.

Hittites were the first to use soap for bathing a thousand years after the invention. Soap was a game changer in getting dirty things clean. But, there is no record of clean bodies or hands improving health during the Bronze Age. In fact, soap for hand washing took so long to catch on, that it is still catching on in many parts of the world. The recent *pandemic* reminded us all the great value of hand washing with soap.

It is possible the Sumerian who invented soap was a woman. Women were the ones who worked in the textile industry. A woman may have been the first to observe what happened during the process of cleaning.

Learn more

> Read **The Dirty History of Soap** from TheConversation.org at: https://theconversation.com/the-dirty-history-of-soap-136434

> Read *Roman Baths and Hygiene in Ancient Rome* from Thoughtco at: https://www.thoughtco.com/hygiene-in-ancient-rome-and-baths-119136

> Read *Who Discovered Soap? What to Know About the Origins of the Life-Saving Substance* from Time magazine at: https://time.com/5831828/soap-origins/.

READING, WRITING, RESEARCH

Level 1

1. What necessity made ancient people want to invent soap? Wood ash, fat, and water seems like a weird mixture to use for cleaning. How did they came up with the idea to use them?

2. In ancient times, they had one kind of soap to clean everything. How many do you have today? Look in every room – bathrooms, kitchen, garage, bedrooms, laundry room – to find as many different types of soap as you can. How many did you find? How many different uses do they have?

3. Look up online to find videos or websites about how soap works. Try kid-friendly search phrases like, "science of lye soap for kids" or "how does soap work kids." Add 'video" or "YouTube" to your phrase if you want to see a video.

Level 2

1. Explain how washing your hands with soap and water can help to keep your whole family healthy.

2. Make up a new brand of soap. Write a commercial script for it. Include the benefits of being clean. You can also write a jingle and design the packaging.

3. *Glycerin* is an ingredient in soaps, cosmetics and many other products today. Research and explain what glycerin is and what its benefits are.

Level 3

1. Research and explain why messy ingredients like fat and wood ash make something that actually takes dirt away. What is the chemical makeup of wood ash? How does that translate to "lye?"

2. Sweating, or perspiration, sets humans apart from animals and has helped us evolve as a species. Research and explain why sweating makes us superior even to four legged runners. For example, how can sweat help us catch an antelope? Do your own research or read about it at: https://www.lesmills.com/us/fit-planet/health/sweat-is-a-good-thing.

STEAM ACTIVITIES AND MORE

Level 1

1. Fill a bin with water and add sand to the bottom. Try washing your dirty hands and feet with only water and sand. Write about your results. How did it feel? How did it work?

2. Make a white towel or article of clothing dirty. Then wash it using these instructions and write what you see after each step: Fill two bins with clean water. First wash the article with only water in one of the bins. Check it and write how clean it got. Next, use a bar of soap to wash it in the same bin. Use the second bin to rinse. Did it get cleaner? Write your answer. Finally, spread the clothing in the sun to dry. Did the sun help to remove any lingering stains? Why might that make a difference?

3. Make soap at home. You can go to your local craft store for a kit; research homemade soaps online or visit: https://www.pbs.org/parents/crafts-and-experiments/how-to-make-soap.

Level 2

1. Lye soap has been a homemaker's primary cleaner for thousands of years. It was actually easy to make using fat, water and lye. Research a recipe for homemade lye soap and try it! Use it to wash toys, the kitchen or bathroom, laundry and even your hands. How well does it work? How different is it from your regular soaps?

2. Do the fun and soapy experiments at: https://lemonlimeadventures.com/soap-experiments-for-kids/. Tell what you learned from them.

3. Put a bar of Ivory® soap on a microwave-safe plate. Microwave on high for 90 seconds. What happened? Note: MUST use Ivory brand soap. May not work with other types of soap. Research 'Charles Law" for the science behind why that happened.

Level 3

1. The reason for washing lanolin out of wool is so you can dye the wool. Find a local source for raw, unwashed wool, or you can buy it online. You can also purchase Fisherman's Wool from your local craft store. Fisherman's wool still contains lanolin to help keep it waterproof. Use soap to wash out the lanolin. Then look up online how to use natural ingredients to dye your wool. For example, visit https://www.smithsonianmag.com/innovation/how-make-clothing-dye-with-excess-fruits-vegetables-from-your-garden-180975720/.

2. Research "how to calculate the lye in soap" online or on YouTube to learn how to create your own lye soap recipe. Then try it!

WORD SEARCH

E	B	T	K	I	P	G	X	N	O	A	M	D	R	M	L	I	W	G
D	Z	P	J	V	A	B	K	E	Y	C	Y	C	L	E	A	N	E	R
I	H	S	M	G	O	E	J	R	H	I	T	T	I	T	E	S	L	H
R	E	T	M	W	S	N	D	A	A	N	I	L	O	N	A	L	O	O
O	Y	R	C	Q	T	N	R	N	I	A	H	P	A	W	Y	F	O	S
L	P	I	H	G	U	L	I	A	V	W	D	I	J	S	F	V	W	O
H	G	G	C	A	E	M	K	V	K	J	R	J	U	T	G	N	S	N
C	G	E	L	S	A	D	M	R	A	E	S	A	E	R	G	O	N	P
O	J	L	L	L	Q	S	B	N	M	Y	A	C	B	X	Y	L	A	Z
R	L	A	F	M	Z	W	I	U	G	C	N	U	Z	C	O	I	M	T
D	W	A	E	P	V	D	S	W	H	N	U	L	S	N	E	V	R	D
Y	T	T	M	A	B	U	S	Q	K	S	I	N	D	K	H	E	E	J
H	Z	G	C	A	K	A	J	R	D	V	A	H	U	H	O	O	H	M
M	Z	S	M	D	L	Y	H	V	Z	O	P	T	T	B	G	I	S	O
U	G	X	X	K	W	Z	K	Y	G	X	N	W	N	A	I	L	I	K
I	R	E	A	N	A	V	C	Q	L	R	H	P	S	A	B	H	F	X
D	R	L	N	T	T	H	F	H	Y	T	E	X	T	I	L	E	S	W
O	I	M	V	S	E	L	U	T	E	Z	V	I	V	L	M	P	H	W
S	W	V	N	I	R	E	C	Y	L	G	A	A	E	G	N	G	M	C

Alkali	Fisherman's wool	Laundry	Sodium hydrochloride
Animal fat	Glycerin	Lye	Strigel
Bathing	Grease	Olive oil	Sumerian
Charles Law	Hittites	Plant ash	Textiles
Cleaner	Lanolin	Soap	Water

COLORING PAGE

INVENTION DISCUSSION PAGE

Name:____Date:_________________

Invention/Product:____

Who invented it?____When?______________

How does it work?

____

____

____

What problem did it solve?

____

____

____

What was it like before the product was invented? What did people use or do instead?

____

____

____

Who could own it? (Did everyone get to use it? Was it expensive? Was it easy to get?)

____

____

____

Can anyone use this product? What skill was needed to operate it?

____

____

____

Is the product still in use today? How has it changed since its original invention?

____

____

____

WEAPONS

1,700 BCE

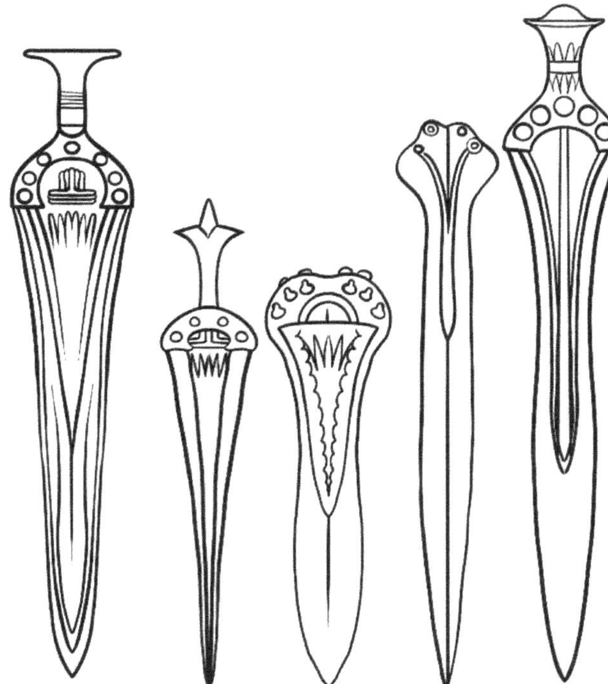

Stone Age people used *weapons* to catch dinner and defend their families from wild *predators*. The Agricultural Revolution resulted in civilizations, social hierarchy, and wealth. As you might imagine, theft and *organized warfare* quickly followed. *Defense* from other humans became a necessity.

The first weapons were the same as those used to kill and skin meat. They included stone hand axes, arrows, and spears. Eventually those tools turned to copper, which allowed for design improvement. A copper arrowhead or skinning knife could inflict harm. But, a bronze *dagger* was much more *lethal*. These arrived on the scene as early as 4,000 BCE. Bronze is easier to mold It's also stronger so you could make the blade longer than a skinning tool.

A *halberd* was a wooden staff with a bronze *blade* at the top. The blade was at a right angle, so it looked like a scythe rather than like a spear. This weapon emerged in Europe around 2,200 BCE. Many used to believe halberds were just for show. But Bronze Age halberds found in Ireland show they were used in combat.

If you've studied Egyptian art, you may have seen armies wielding a deadly weapon called the *khopesh*. The blade is shaped like a sickle – or a dog's leg, as its Egyptian name implies. Unlike a sickle, the blade is on the curved outside for slashing enemies instead of the inside for cutting wheat.

Daggers eventually evolved into *swords* by 1,700 BCE near the Aegean and southeastern Europe. After 1,400 BCE, swords spread out to Central Europe, Britain, India, and Asia. Swords were good for hand-to-hand combat because they had a longer reach than daggers. Plus swords could slice where a dagger was meant for stabbing.

Even after swords were invented, many armies continued to rely on *spears* and *arrows* for their main weapons. They were faster and cheaper to mass produce since only the tip was made of metal. A sword had to be cast as one solid piece, from *hilt* to blade, to make it stronger. Swords were not economical to a large army.

With all these new weapons, warriors needed protection. *Shields* came first but no one really knows when. The wood and leather shields were biodegradable and might not have lasted for us to find later. During the later Bronze Age, they discovered that hammering a flat piece of bronze gave it strength. So they started adding a layer of bronze between the wood to make their shields stronger.

The advent of iron around the first millennium BCE quickly put bronze weaponry out of business. Everything was stronger with iron!

Learn more

➢ Read about *Bronze Age Weapons* from History.com at: https://www.history.com/news/bronze-age-weapons.

➢ Read *Prehistoric warfare* from Wikipedia at: https://en.wikipedia.org/wiki/Prehistoric_warfare#Chalcolithic_to_Bronze_Age

➢ Learn about the *Talheim Death Pit* from Wikipedia at: https://en.wikipedia.org/wiki/Talheim_Death_Pit

➢ Learn about the *Halberd* from Wikipedia at: https://en.wikipedia.org/wiki/Halberd.

➢ Read *9 Blades that Forged History* from History.com at: https://www.history.com/news/knives-that-changed-history.

➢ Read *Bronze Age Warfare: Manufacture and Use of Weaponry* by O'Flaherty, Ronan at: https://www.academia.edu/1640588/Ceremonial_or_deadly_serious_Function_of_Irish_EBA_halberds.

➢ Learn about the **Bronze Age Collapse** from WorldHistory.org at: https://www.worldhistory.org/Bronze_Age_Collapse/.

READING, WRITING, RESEARCH

Level 1

1. Write about or tell why you think people started to fight wars after they settled in civilizations?

2. Visit a local museum that has ancient weapons. Learn what time period and civilizations the weapons are from. You can also search online for museum displays of weapons.

3. Research "Bronze Age Sword." Identify the different parts of a sword. Which part protects the hand?

Level 2

1. Search on "Bronze Age Spear Fighting video" or visit: https://youtu.be/2gctjLzCF4I to learn how Bronze Age warriors in Britain fought using a spear and shield.

2. A halberd of the Bronze Age was a pole with a knife stuck at 90 degrees on the end. Research "halberd" of the Middle Ages and discuss how they differ from halberd of the Bronze Age.

3. Pretend you're a Bronze Age soldier going into battle. Which weapon do you want to have with you and why? Compare and discuss with someone who chose differently.

Level 3

1. Read *Warrior Scarlett* by Rosemary Sutcliff. Support why the tribe rejected Drem. If he only has one good arm and cannot hold a shield and sword at the same time, how did he ultimately becomes a warrior?

2. Research possible reasons for the 5,500 BCE battle that took place at the excavation site of the *Talheim Death Pit* in Germany? What were the people fighting over? How do researchers know this?

3. Watch the video at https://youtu.be/6rn9b7Z1ZnQ which is a history of Mesopotamia. It explains how the Gutians conquered the Akkadians and integrated into their culture. This behavior has been repeated again and again throughout history from other conquerors. Consider and discuss why an army would attack and defeat a civilization only to adopt their way of life.

4. The Bronze Age collapsed around 1,200 BCE. That was right at the start of the Iron Age. Major cities and civilizations fell, trade ended, and writing systems vanished. Different theories exist from natural disasters, to invasions to climate change. Research the different reasons and support the one you think was most impactful in a written or oral report. Remember to cite your sources. You can also have a formal debate if someone chooses differently.

STEAM ACTIVITIES AND MORE

Level 1

1. Design, draw, and color a sword with all four of the parts you learned about on page 61.

2. Look up how to make a paper spear or visit: https://www.wikihow.com/Make-a-Paper-Spear. Then make one!

3. All weapons require practice. You can practice aiming and hitting a target to reach regular success. Use lawn darts, a baseball to a catcher, bottle caps at a magnet, or simply set up a tin can and throw stones at it. If you miss your target, think about how you can adjust to improve your aim. Be safe! Make sure no one is between you and your target.

Level 2

1. Armor must protect your body while also allowing freedom of movement. Design armor for yourself or a doll using cardboard, faux leather, padding, and other materials. Decorate your armor to scare your enemies.

2. Take an archery class to learn proper techniques. Or look up online and practice in your yard. How well can you do? Challenge others to a contest.

3. Make a strong, layered cardboard shield. Also make a spear out of a long strait pole or stick, and a safe cardboard tip. Practice the techniques you learned in the video in level 2 #1 on page 61.

Level 3

1. Watch the video on "Bronze Age Spear Fighting video" at https://youtu.be/2gctjLzCF4I. Explain how the figure 8 design makes a shield stronger. Create a model of a similar shield to replicate the strength of the Figure 8 design.

2. Design a wax sword. Using a fine damp silt or sand in a box, design a sword, including the pommel, handle, guard, and blade. You can make it as fancy as you like. Pour in melted soy, bees, or paraffin wax and allow it to harden. Display your masterpiece.

3. Read about shields and armor at https://www.history.com/news/bronze-age-weapons. Purchase one machine-cut flat bronze disc or square, and one ingot of bronze. Leave the machine-cut piece as purchased. Beat the ingot with a hammer or mallet into a flat shape. Try to pierce both flat pieces with a semi-sharp point such as a knitting needle. What was the result? Was one stronger than the other? [Search online for "bronze for sale" or "bronze ingots" to find an inexpensive source.]

CROSSWORD PUZZLE

Across:

2 Stabbing weapon

6 A person trained for warfare

8 Egyptian sickle-shaped weapon

12 Long dangerous part of a sword

13 Military land forces

14 Handle of a sword

15 Bronze Age pole with a knife at the end

16 To keep safe from an enemy

18 Protective covering

Down:

1 Planned group conflict

3 Worn on forearm to ward off blows

4 Pointed tip of an arrow

5 Tool for cutting grain with long blade and curved handle

7 Armed battle

8 Knob on the end of the hilt of a sword

10 Weapon with long shaft and sharp point

11 Tool used for hunting, fighting or eating

17 Hand weapon with long blade

COLORING PAGE

INVENTION DISCUSSION PAGE

Name:____Date:________________

Invention/Product:____

Who invented it?____When?___________

How does it work?

____

____

____

What problem did it solve?

____

____

____

What was it like before the product was invented? What did people use or do instead?

____

____

____

Who could own it? (Did everyone get to use it? Was it expensive? Was it easy to get?)

____

____

____

Can anyone use this product? What skill was needed to operate it?

____

____

____

Is the product still in use today? How has it changed since its original invention?

____

____

____

TIMEKEEPER

1,600 BCE

The very first clocks were the sun and moon. Time was either daytime or nighttime. You could follow the sun across the sky to reasonably tell how long you had until night came.

As people settled into civilizations, their lives became more routine and it became important to measure the hours. There were many reasons to know the time. A laborer wanted to know when it was quitting time. A leader needed to know his meeting time. A cook needed to know when to have a meal ready. Enter the timekeeper around 1,600 BCE.

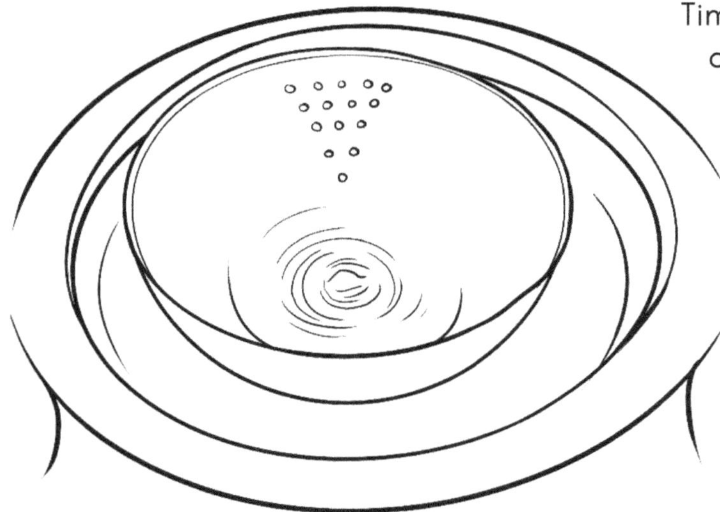

Drawing of ancient Persian water clock.

The oldest type of clock is a *water clock*. This measures time either by flowing water into the container (inflow) or flowing water out of a container (outflow) at a controlled speed. Water clocks used markers to note the passage of time based on how much water was in the container. Different types of water clocks were made during the Bronze Age in China, Egypt, Babylon, Persia, India, Greece, and Rome.

Egyptians made the earliest known *sundial* around 1,500 BCE. It was a clay tablet with a drawn half circle marked into twelve sections.

A *gnomon* is the part that casts the shadow. The Egyptians even used a tall obelisk as a gnomon in a giant sundial.

After the Bronze Age, timekeeping became more sophisticated. The Chinese invented the *candle clock*, which was designed to burn and melt at a specific speed. You could tell how much time had passed by the markings on the remaining wax.

The *hourglass* and *mechanical clocks* were products of the Middle Ages. But, even as recent as two hundred years ago, the sundial remained one of humanity's primary methods of telling time.

Learn more

- ➢ Learn the *History of Timekeeping* from Wikipedia at: https://en.wikipedia.org/wiki/History_of_timekeeping_devices .

- ➢ Read about *Water Clock* from Wikipedia at: https://en.wikipedia.org/wiki/Water_clock.

- ➢ Read *A Walk Through Time – Early Clocks* from the National Institutes of Standards and Technology at: https://www.nist.gov/pml/time-and-frequency-division/popular-links/walk-through-time/walk-through-time-early-clocks.

- ➢ Learn about *The World's Oldest Working Clock* from Experience Salsbury at: https://www.experiencesalisbury.co.uk/salisbury-blog/2021/june/the-world-s-oldest-working-clock/

READING, WRITING, RESEARCH

Level 1

1. Read *The Warlord's Alarm* by Virginia Pilegard. Was Chuan and Jing Jing's Chinese clock an inflow or outflow type of water clock? Look up and read about Persian water clocks and tell which kind (inflow or outflow) they used.

2. Name three reasons why ancient people wanted to measure time. Name three reasons why you or other members of your family measure time today. Are any of your reasons the same as the ancient people's reasons? How are they different?

3. Talk about how ancient people kept track of time. Did everyone have access to the time? Compare that to today. Go around your home and count how many devices tell you the time. Is there a place in your home where you cannot see the time? Which room(s) are those? Why or why not?

Level 2

1. Research and explain how the two different types of water clocks (inflow and outflow) worked.

2. You can thank the ancient Mesopotamians for the base 60, sexagesimal system. Look up online or visit: https://en.m.wikipedia.org/wiki/sexagesimal/. Explain how we still use the sexagesimal system in timekeeping today.

3. Do you think measuring time is more important or less important to us than it was to the ancient people? What clues led you to your answer?

Level 3

1. Learn about sundials at: https://www.homestratosphere.com/types-of-sundials/. Someone who lives in the north (where the sun is lower in the sky part of the year) can be in the same time zone as someone who lives in the south (where the sun is usually higher in the sky). Explain how can a sundial tell the same time for both places? What about those who live east and west in different time zones?

2. Have a philosophical discussion with someone about time or debate your answers with someone who disagrees. Here are some questions:

   ➤ Which is more valuable – time or money? Why do you think so?

   ➤ If you have all the time in the world, what would you fill it with? Why? In ten years, would you wish you had picked differently? What about fifty years? A hundred years?

   ➤ Would you rather have work you enjoy or lots of time to do nothing? Why?

STEAM ACTIVITIES AND MORE

Level 1

1. Search on "DIY Hourglass." Choose a method you like and make one. Is it an hourglass, a minute glass, or some other length of time? Test it against a stop watch and adjust so it empties in the correct amount of time.

2. Search on "DIY Sundial' or visit https://www.pbs.org/parents/crafts-and-experiments/diy-sundial to learn how to make a sundial. Then make one! Check your sundial on a sunny day to see if you can tell the time with it.

3. Visit a museum and look for different timepieces. Ask a guide to explain when and where they are from. Which one is the oldest? As an alternative, you can visit https://www.sciencemuseum.org.uk/see-and-do/clockmakers-museum. Look for the oldest one. Where is it from? When was it made? Who made it? Do the math to see how many years it was made after the oldest water clock (1,600 BCE).

Level 2

1. Learn how to build a Babylonian sundial at http://www.space-awareness.org/bg/activities/6048/build-a-babylonian-sundial/. Discuss how the Earth's rotation is related to the movement of time. Invent a weather resistant sundial that uses a gnomon. Find a place for it in your yard or garden to use throughout the year.

2. How many seconds are in an hour? How many minutes are in a day? As an added challenge, can you calculate the number of days that have passed during your lifetime? Remember to adjust for leap years.

3. Learn how you can make a water clock with the four-part video at the Children's Museum of Indianapolis. Then try to build your own water clock using simple items from around your home.

> Episode 1: https://youtu.be/ahu3uLul5qo.
> Episode 2: https://youtu.be/Nkz2uoNY8ZM
> Episode 3: https://youtu.be/ChJ7vl6e9D0
> Episode 4: https://youtu.be/Of6JVF601RA

Level 3

1. The oldest way to tell time was by the sun. Learn how at: https://www.wikihow.com/Tell-Time-Without-a-Clock. Spend a day outside with someone else. You have no access to a clock. The other person does. Throughout the day, you declare the time based on the sun's position. The other person records your guess along with the accurate time. At the end of the day, see how well you did.

2. Explore how to keep time and what makes a 'good' clock. Visit: https://wonders.physics.wisc.edu/build-your-own-clock/. Try making your own working clock as shown on the website. You will need to review the Teacher Materials list first and purchase any necessary items.

HOURGLASS MAZE

COLORING PAGE

INVENTION DISCUSSION PAGE

Name:____Date:_________________

Invention/Product:____

Who invented it?____When?___________

How does it work?

____

____

____

What problem did it solve?

____

____

____

What was it like before the product was invented? What did people use or do instead?

____

____

____

Who could own it? (Did everyone get to use it? Was it expensive? Was it easy to get?)

____

____

____

Can anyone use this product? What skill was needed to operate it?

____

____

____

Is the product still in use today? How has it changed since its original invention?

____

____

____

PUZZLE SOLUTIONS

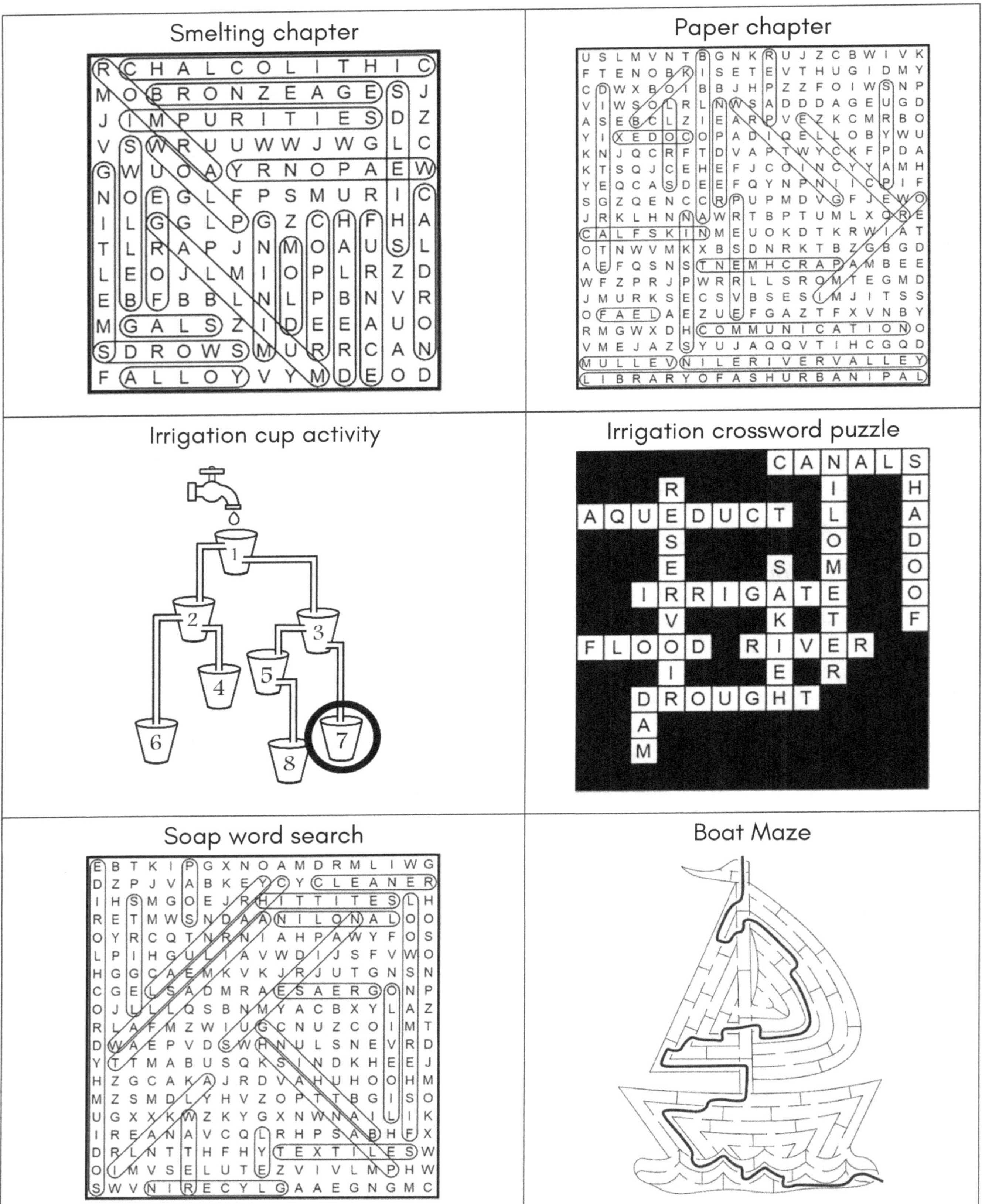

Smelting chapter

Paper chapter

Irrigation cup activity

Irrigation crossword puzzle

Soap word search

Boat Maze

Boat Word Search

Weapons crossword puzzle

Hourglass maze

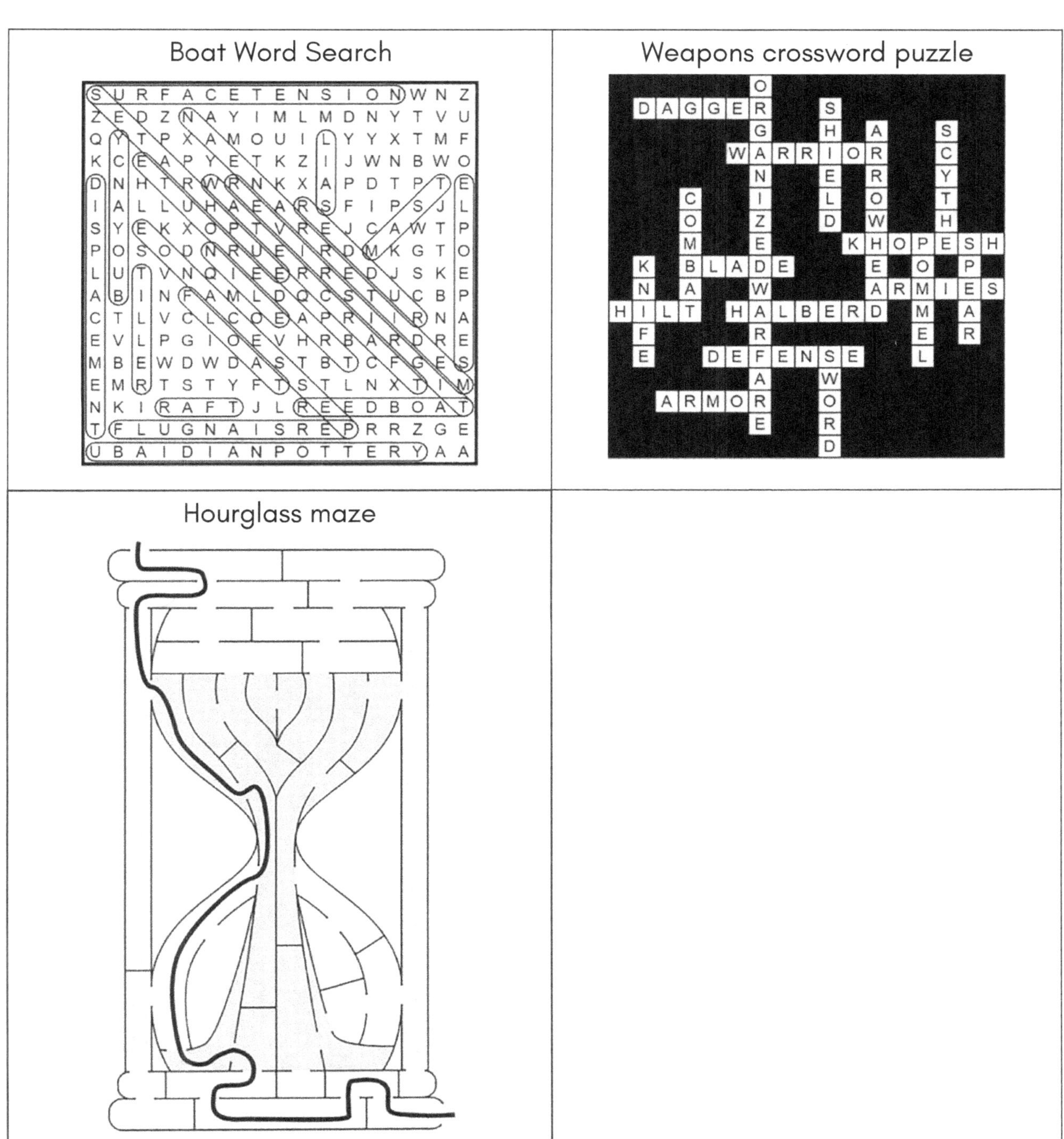